By the same author

THE TRANSATLANTIC MAIL

Plate 1. A comical cartoon by John Leech inspired by the introduction of uniform penny postage—

"Is this the General Post, Sir?"

"Yes, Mum."

"Then will you just have the goodness to stamp upon my little boy here, and send him off to Gravesend!"

THE PENNY POST
1680-1918

by
FRANK STAFF

THE LUTTERWORTH PRESS

CAMBRIDGE

The Lutterworth Press
P.O. Box 60
Cambridge
CB1 2NT

British Library Cataloguing-in-Publication Data
A catalogue record for this book is available from the British Library

ISBN 0-7188-2878-X

Copyright © 1964 Frank Staff

First Published by The Lutterworth Press 1964
First paperback edition 1992

Printed in Great Britain
by St Edmundsbury Press

Contents

CHAPTERS

Appendices

Figures

List of Illustrations

PLATES

Introduction

MY STORY describes the struggle fought by public-spirited men through the centuries against what seemed to be insurmountable odds, in order that the people of these islands might benefit from improved postal services and lower postage rates.

The British Post Office, with its long and romantic story, has reason to be proud of its great tradition and organization, but few people are aware that many of its improvements have come about through the initiative and ideas of individuals outside its administration.

The Penny Post originated as a private undertaking in the seventeenth century. By the beginning of this present century its usefulness had spread to many parts of the world. Today we no longer have a penny postage in any shape or form, but although the prospects of a return to a cheaper postage would appear remote and impossible, they are no more impossible than circumstances allowed in days gone by.

Thanks to postal historians and the keen interest taken in the study and collecting of old letters and postal markings, we have a comprehensive picture of the whole Penny Post story.

In writing this book I have been greatly helped by the attention and patience shown me by Mr. Thomas and his staff of the G.P.O. records room. Likewise my thanks are due to several whose names are not known to me in the British Museum reading room and the Guildhall Library, also the library of the Victoria and Albert Museum.

I owe special thanks to Mr. T. Todd, who has allowed me to use freely the interesting information contained in his book *William Dockwra and the Rest of the Undertakers*. I am likewise indebted to The Bodley Head Ltd., publishers of Mrs. Adrian Porter's book *The Life and Letters of Sir John Henniker Heaton, Bart.*, who also granted permission for the reproduction of Plate 18*a*. I have had considerable help from articles on the Peter Williamson story written by Professor Sir Walter Mercer of Edinburgh, and I am grateful to Mary C. Hill, who has allowed me to refer to her book *The King's Messengers 1199–1377* (Edward Arnold).

My thanks also to Mr. Foster Bond, who has painstakingly checked on many points for me, and to Mr. Elliott Perry of West-field, New Jersey, who is a leading authority on the private and local posts of the United States.

Other postal historians to whom thanks are due are Mr. Robson Lowe, Mr. Sydney Raine, Mr. F. E. Dixon, Mr. J. A. Dennett, Mr. C. Hall, Dr. D. Patton and Mr. Charles Calvert; and in America to Mr. Wm. C. Peterman, of Caldwell, New Jersey, and Mr. Henry Abt of New York.

To the following I make grateful acknowledgement for use of illustrations:

To H.M. Postmaster General, for permission to reproduce the portrait of Sir Rowland Hill (Plate 7*a*) and to illustrate the handbill of 1890 (Fig. 38).

To the National Portrait Gallery for permission to reproduce the portrait of Sir Henry Cole (Plate 7*b*).

To the Guildhall Library for permission to illustrate the postal broadside of 1652 (Fig. 4) and Dockwra's Penny Post notice of 1680 (Fig. 7).

To the Victoria and Albert Museum for permission to illustrate two items from the Henry Cole Bequest (Plates 8*b* and 10).

To the Trustees of the British Museum for permission to illustrate the postal broadsheet of 1635 (Fig. 2), the title page of John Hill's pamphlet (Fig. 3), and the Dockwra handbill of 1681 (Fig. 8).

To the Proprietors of *Punch* for permission to reproduce the cartoon "Advance Australia" (Fig. 23).

To *The News of the World* for permission to reproduce the Imperial Penny Postage cartoon of 1898 (Fig. 22).

To Mr. John A. Fox of New York for permission to illustrate the Northern Liberties Newsrooms cover (Plate 13*a*).

To Mr. Gerald Wellburn of Duncan, B.C., for permission to illustrate the New York Cheap Postage Association envelope (Plate 23*b*).

To Mr. G. B. Horton for permission to illustrate the Ocean Penny Postage letter sheet (Fig. 19).

To Mr. Foster Bond for the use of his Penny Post notice of 1908 (Fig. 24).

October 1963   FRANK W. STAFF,
                                                   West Bay, Bridport

CHAPTER 1

The Start of a System

MEDIAEVAL POSTAL SERVICES—MESSENGERS AND POST BOYS—
THOMAS WITHERINGS ORGANIZES A SYSTEM—POSTAL RATES
FIRST SETTLED—EDMUND PRIDEAUX—PRIVATE UNDERTAKINGS
—A PENNY POST SUGGESTED IN 1659—THE ACT OF 1660—
HENRY BISHOP AND MAJOR WILDMAN

IT WAS DURING 1680 that two citizens of London started an enterprise which was to have far-reaching consequences, and thanks to the initiative and the persistent agitation of a few public-spirited men some two hundred years later, these consequences completely changed our whole postal system, and affected our social life. For the outcome of it all was a Penny Postal system, which operated not only throughout the length and breadth of the British Isles but reached to many parts of the world as well.

With the rebuilding of London after the Great Fire of 1666, there was a very considerable increase in her trade. The City became the commercial centre of business, which was not only expanding within the kingdom but in Europe as well. Still farther afield our West Indian colonies were beginning to prosper, as well as the plantations in the New England States, now part of the United States of America. Necessary to trade and business, no matter on what scale, whether it be that of a big merchant or of a small tradesman, is speedy communication and a well-organized postal service. This was not available, and was a continual source of complaint on the part of the merchants and businessmen alike.

On looking at the story of the development of our postal services, they seem to have begun in a haphazard way; particularly when compared with the highly efficient posts in some of the continental countries. A thousand years had gone by since the days of the *cursus publicus* of the Roman occupation, the Itinerary of Antoninus,[1] and any roads worthy of the name. It was not until 1482 that horsemen were stationed approximately every twenty miles so that letters could be carried to and from London when the king was dealing with his troubles in the North.

In the fifteenth century, in order to send a letter, people had to find their own means. There were the regular "common carriers" of goods, and sometimes a traveller, or maybe a soldier going in the right direction, might be found who could be relied on to deliver the letter; unless of course it was possible to send one's own servant. Many contemporary letters are to be found mentioning the means employed in sending them. Elizabeth Stonor, writing to her cousin in 1476, says, "And, Sir, as this day by your servant Thomas Mathew I received a letter from you, by which letter I understand . . ."

Carriers are sometimes recommended. Margaret Paston wrote,[2] "If it please you to send anything by the bearer hereof, he is trusty enough." Sometimes it was difficult; John Paston's younger son wrote to his brother from Newcastle, "I send no letter to my father, ever since I departed from you, for I could get no man to London." It seems messengers were usually paid before setting out, but references to payments are scanty.

The Church, too, had a postal system which had developed from earliest times, as well as the Universities, whose messengers went from one city to another throughout the land.

Royal letters and letters of State were carried by the King's Messengers, a small select company of couriers who are mentioned in the State papers of our country as early as the reign of King John, when they are referred to as nuncii or cursores.[3] They carried a bag

---

[1] *Commentary on Antoninus*, by Wm. Burton, pub. 1658. An account of the itinerary and travels of Antoninus "of the Romane Empire so far as it concerneth Britain".

[2] *The Pastons and their England*, Bennett. An analysis of seventy-four cases of Paston family letters in which any mention is made of the messenger gives the following results: 44 messengers mentioned by name, 16 as the retainers of known folk, 14 vague references such as "the bearer", "the next messenger", etc.

[3] A nuncius was a mounted messenger in the permanent employment of the King. A cokinus was a servant employed as a foot messenger and is first mentioned in documents dating from 1272. Later "cokini" were referred to as "cursores", a name which became more popular. *The King's Messengers, 1199–1377*, Mary C. Hill (Edward Arnold).

for letters emblazoned with the Royal Arms,[1] suspended from the belt, and became a familiar sight along the roads throughout the country. Sometimes a box was carried, instead of a pouch or bag. Chaucer, in his *Hous of Fame*, refers to "Currours and eke messangers with boistes". The ancient name Knight-rider, which dates from mediaeval times, is possibly connected with them, or with heralds, who have always been messengers of the sovereign. It survives today as the name of a small street close to the Heralds' college in the vicinity of St. Paul's Cathedral.

During the reign of King Henry VIII the King's Messengers were re-organized under a court official, Sir Brian Tuke, the first official to hold this position. Tuke was French Secretary to the King (as well as holding other offices) and well acquainted with communications to the Continent and the posts that were being organized there. He was, therefore, well suited to set up and to superintend a system for carrying the King's letters. The title and date of Tuke's appointment is not found upon the Rolls, but it was about the year 1512 when he was referred to as "Master of the Posts".[2]

A route where a post was to be "laid" was divided into stages of 10–20 miles; and at each stage someone was made responsible for having horses and "posts" always in readiness. This system of post stages was used in two ways. A King's Messenger riding "in Commission" would take the letter or packet, with which he was entrusted, all the way. This method being known as the "through post". If, on the other hand, the letter or packet changed hands on the way, it went by what was known as the "standing post", which was in readiness to carry letters forward to the next stage. This was the faster method over long distances, and was used for "Express Letters". We hear of serious defects and complaints made to Tuke in connection with his endeavours.

To have a clear appreciation of the story of the posts that were now developing, it is essential to bear in mind a particular feature that played a most important part in the early history of our postal

---

[1] The Royal Arms continued to be the insignia for the Royal Messengers for nearly 600 years, when they were replaced by the Royal Monogram in the reign of King Edward VII.

[2] Letters and Papers, Foreign and Domestic, Henry VIII.ii, pt. 2, p. 1454.

services. Attention, therefore, must be drawn to the Secretaries of State. These officers of the Crown were responsible for obtaining all the information possible concerning enemy countries as well as any domestic plots, and in addition to this every kind of news was sought. Bearing this in mind, it can be understood how it was very soon realized that any kind of correspondence could be of great use if it could be made to pass through the hands of the Secretaries of State or their appointed agent.[1] The importance of this is borne out by a brief study of the appointments and activities of Tuke and his successors.

During the reign of Elizabeth I there is evidence that the Royal Messengers sometimes carried unofficial and private letters, a custom that gradually became general, although it was expressly forbidden in the instructions given in "The Directions for the Post", which appeared in the last year of the Queen's reign.[2]

Towards the end of the sixteenth century trade with the Continent, and particularly with the Low Countries, was rapidly growing. The English Merchant Adventurers, and their overseas equivalent the Merchant Strangers, organized their own postal service, employing their own men. The Queen was determined to see that such letters passed through official channels, and a proclamation of 1591 made it clear that she intended to enforce this. Thus began the seemingly endless struggle for the control of the posts for foreign parts. A control which was not entirely gained until 1632.

In that year Thomas Witherings and William Frizell were appointed "Masters of the Posts for Foreign Parts". They soon quarrelled, however, and Witherings took sole control. He was well acquainted with the Court and with conditions on the Continent, and was a very suitable man. In addition to the merchant's letters, he organized the carriage of ordinary private letters.

As a result of the success of his efforts in the control of the posts, he was ordered to go ahead and link up the overseas posts with all parts of the United Kingdom. This plan was established

[1] Anyone writing the early history of our Intelligence Service would at the same time be writing an account of the beginning of our postal services.

[2] Four Tudor Posts came to be regarded as permanent; they were known as "The Court to Dover, The Court to Plymouth, The Court to Berwick, and the Court to Beaumaris". The posts were expected to do seven miles per hour in the summer and five miles per hour in the winter.

A
Straunge Foot-Poſt,
VVith
A Packet full of ſtrange
Petitions
After a long Vacation for a good Terme.

Printed at London by E. A. dwelling neare
Chriſt-Church. 1613.

Fig. 1. *The title page of this rare book shows the dress of a foot-post in 1613.*

in 1635 by a Royal Proclamation "for settling the Letter Office of England and Scotland". It was the beginning of our postal services.

Witherings was given the right to settle "a running post or two" to run night and day on the routes out of London to Edinburgh, Norwich, Chester and Holyhead, Bristol and Plymouth, with branch posts from the main routes. The proclamation established postal rates. Twopence was charged up to 80 miles, from 80 to 140 miles, fourpence, and above 140 miles, sixpence, into Scotland, eightpence, and to Ireland, ninepence. These charges were for a single letter, that is to say, for one sheet of paper only. Two sheets or pieces of paper would be double postage and three sheets treble, and so on. Anything in the nature of a wrapper or envelope counted as an extra sheet of paper and would be charged accordingly, so were rarely used. The letter sheet was folded and usually sealed with wax, with space being left for the directions or address. Pre-payment was optional, but it was usually left for the recipient to pay the post, thus ensuring safe delivery of the letter.

The posts, or messengers, set out from London on appointed days of the week with a bag of letters for the post towns on their routes. The roads throughout the country were not roads as visualized today. They were much more like farm tracks, wide in places where the "traffic" had deviated to avoid holes and soft pieces of ground. The provincial postmasters were usually the keepers of the principal inns, which were very important establishments in those days, and were under orders to keep horses constantly ready for the government posts. They also kept additional horses to be let to travellers "riding post" from one stage to the next, and some of them were bitterly opposed to providing horses for Witherings's messengers as well as for the carriage of the King's Mail. In those days post horses and letter carrying belonged one to the other, and postmasters were those who kept horses to be let for riding post, or for travellers riding with the post.

Not all messengers rode on horseback. The foot-post, besides being the oldest form of messenger, was still the commonest to be met with on the roads, and it was natural that he should be included in the postal organization. When he was on official duties he wore a badge showing the Royal Arms, and like the horse messengers,

❧ To all people to whom this preſent
Declaration may concerne.

Hereas his Majeſtie by his Proclamation, dated at *Bagſhot*, the laſt day of *Iuly*, 1635. hath for the advancement of the Correſpondencie of all his loving Subjects, commanded his Servant, *Thomas Withrings* Eſquire, to ſettle a Running Poſt, to goe and returne every weeke, betwixt the Citie of *London* and *Holy-head* in *Wales*, and from thence to the Citie of *Dublin* in *Ireland*, and ſo to all parts of the Kingdome of *Ireland*, as the ſaid Letters ſhall be directed, and anſwers return'd (if the Winds ſerve, in ſixe dayes) if not, howſoever in ſixe dayes betweene *Holyhead* and *London*. And ſhall begin to goe on Tueſday next, being the 3. of *November*, at 8. of the clocke at night ; and ſo to continue to goe every Tueſday night, at 8. a clocke, throughout the yeere ; and Anſwers to be returned on every Monday night afterwards conſtantly ; and ſhall be then ready to take with him, the Letters of Saint *Albans*, *Dunſtable*, *Brick-bill*, *Stony-Straiford*, *Dauentry*, *Couentry*, *Tamworth*, *Litchfield*, *Stafford*, *Stone*, *Nantwitch*, *Cheſter*, *Flint*, *Rutland*, *Aberconway*, *Beaumarice*, *Holy-head*, and all ſuch other places, as are upon this Road , or neere this Road : which Letters and Anſwers, are to be brought, and received, at the Houſe of the ſaid *Thomas Withrings*, in *Sherborne Lane*, neere *Lumbard-ſtreet*, in *London*. And that every man may the better know what Port to pay for the ſaid Letters ; I thought fit (according to his Maieſties ſaid Proclamation) to give notice that the Money is to be paid at the Compting Houſe of the ſaid *Thomas Withrings*, both at the receipt and delivery of the Anſwers of the ſaid Letters, and nothing to be paid in the Country, as followeth ; two pence the ſingle Letter, if under 80. miles ; if between 80. and 140. miles, foure pence ; if above 140. miles, ſixe pence for the Letters of *Ireland*, that goe to *Dublin*, according to the Proclamation, already proclaimed in *Ireland*, are there to pay nine pence the ſingle Letter ; if above, two ſhillings, ſixe pence by the ounce, if they goe further than *Dublin*, then to pay here free to *Dublin* ; and for ſuch as ſhall be returned from any place in *Ireland* to *London*, to pay here nine pence the ſingle Letter ; if above two ſhillings ſixe pence the ounce, which Letters, as before, are to be ſent forward every Tueſday night, and Anſwers received every Monday night. And by the ſaid Proclamation, his Maieſtie hath further ſignified his Royall pleaſure, That from the beginning of this ſervice or imployment, no other Meſſenger or Meſſengers, Foot-Poſt or Foot-Poſts, ſhall take up, carry, receive, or deliver any Letter or Letters whatſoever, other than the Meſſengers appointed by the ſaid *Thomas Withrings*, to any ſuch place or places as the ſaid *Thomas Withrings* ſhall ſettle the conveyances, as aforeſaid. All which his Maieſtie, by his ſaid Proclamation, hath ſtraightly charged and commanded all his loving Subiects whatſoever, duly to obſerve his Royall pleaſure therein declared, as they will anſwer the contrary at their perils.

Printed by *E. P.* at the Inſtance of the ſaid *Tho. Withrings*, his Majeſties Poſt-Maſter for forraigne parts : And are to be ſold at the Shop of *Nicholas Bourne* Stationer, at the South-Entrance of the *Royall Exchange*, in *London*.

M. C. D. XXXV.

Fig. 2. *The famous broadsheet of 1635 announcing that Thomas Witherings will "settle a Running Post". In this notice rates of postage were given for the first time. (Courtesy, The Trustees of the British Museum.)*

carried a horn, which he sounded to announce his arrival or to warn of his approach.

Messengers, or "post-boys" as they were now called, were not always the brightest and smartest of individuals, and they were not boys in the accepted meaning. They were sometimes the worse for liquor, and it was complained on one occasion that "the gentry doe give much money to the riders, whereby they be very subject to get in liquor, which stopes the mails". Their horses have been described as old nags, for not every provincial postmaster provided his best horses for the posts; and it was not unknown for a postmaster to take a horse from its work in the field and harness it for the use of the post-boy. But very likely the poor accounts which have been handed down to us about the post-boys and their horses refer only to a few. For it is well known that bad news is repeated more readily than good, so that it is unfair to generalize.

Certainly the romantic expression "Haste, Post Haste", sometimes written on the front of a letter, would not refer to such as these, but to the King's Messengers, the word post meaning the person or carrier. Important letters were often endorsed "Haste, Post Haste, For Life, For Life" stressing their importance, and the custom of writing "Haste, Post Haste", used mainly by people in authority, gradually died out during the seventeenth century. If a private person wished to emphasize a letter's urgency the words "with speed" were usually added.

Witherings's organization, although somewhat primitive, was none the less a wonderful improvement, for the custom of sending letters by servants or by the carrier still prevailed in just the same way as it did 150 years before. Thomas Reynell, writing to his father in Devon from Exeter College, Oxford, in June 1603, began, "Dear Father, my humble dutye remembred, having so fitt a messenger as this Carriar Sanders I thought good to troubel you with these few lines. . . ."

The new plan went into operation in 1637, and some regular posts were established, but there was little or no enthusiasm on the part of the public in general, and people looked with some resentment and suspicion on the government enterprise, having to place their letters into the hands of men employed by the State. A very considerable proportion of the public continued to use the old methods of sending their letters, many preferring to use the provincial carriers, who called at various taverns at least once a week.[1]

In this same year, John Taylor, the doggerel poet and busybody, compiled a *Carrier's Cosmographie* listing available services with a lot of useful information, having references to foot-posts, described in the picturesque style of those days:

> There doth come from Saffron Market in Norfolk a Foot Post who lodgeth at the *Chequer* in Holborn.
> There is a Foot Post that doth come every second Thursday from Nottingham. He lodgeth at the *Swan* in St. John's Street.
> There is a Foot Post from Walsingham that doth come to the *Cross-keys* in Holborn every second Thursday.

And a weekly post for Scotland was arranged:

> Those that will send any letter to Edinburgh, that so they may be conveyed to and from any parts of the kingdom of Scotland, the Post doth lodge at the sign of the *King's Arms* (or the *Cradle*) at the upper end of Cheapside: from whence, every Monday, any that have occasion may send.

In conclusion the final paragraph mentions the General Post Office:

> All those that will send letters to the most parts of the habitable world, or to any parts of our King of Great Britain's Dominions; let them repair to the General Post Master Thomas Witherings at his house in Sherburne Lane, near Abchurch.

A continual source of trouble to Witherings were the private posts which operated from one town to another. Some of these, organized by mayors and corporations, had been long established. They interfered greatly with his revenue, and he experienced difficulty in suppressing them. Reference to these municipal posts is scanty, but we hear of the one established between Exeter and Barnstaple. The city of Hull had a weekly post to London and strongly resisted Witherings's orders to close, so that he threatened to take the case before the Lords of the Privy Council. The letter

---

[1] Such a carrier was Hobson of Cambridge, who died in 1631 a rich man. His name is for ever linked with the word "choice". Hobson carried the mails and ran a livery stable, and made it a rule never to work one horse more than another, so that anyone wishing to hire a horse from his stable was always given the next horse waiting its turn, hence—Hobson's Choice.

carriers of Ipswich and Norwich were imprisoned for violating his monopoly. In 1641 the Mayor and Corporation of Maidstone (who had employed messengers officially since 1562) established a municipal post to London three times a week, permitting only recognized messengers to carry letters against a fine of 10*s.*, so as to discourage the great number of unauthorized persons and "men of irregular life who took to this kind of life".[1]

Individuals also carried letters. We hear of Samuel Jude, a London tradesman, commonly known as "The Travelling Post", who arranged to carry the letters of merchants between London and Plymouth in fourteen days, an early example of private enterprise in postal matters.[2]

During this period of our history civil war and disorder led to confusion in all efforts at administration. No one holding an official appointment could be sure of remaining long in the Royal favour, or could keep clear of the political vicissitudes of those days. Charles Stanhope, whose office of "Post-Master General" had been confirmed by the Attorney General,[3] was commanded to surrender his patent in 1637, the joint Secretaries of State taking over that Office. This was unfortunate because Stanhope now accused Witherings of certain abuses, as a result of which this very able administrator had to relinquish his Office in 1640. There then followed a decade during which the postal services can only be described as being in a state of chaos. Witherings's place was taken by a naturalized foreigner named Burlamachi, who had given some financial assistance to the King. He did not last long, for in 1642 Parliament seized the London Office and dismissed him.

The assignees of Witherings and Burlamachi were the Earl of Warwick and Edmund Prideaux, who were supported by the Lords and Commons respectively. Each endeavoured to seize control of the letters and of the London Office by force. Prideaux succeeded and was recognized by Parliament in 1644.[4] He, like Witherings,

---

[1] It is interesting to note that this post was organized almost immediately after Witherings's fall in 1640, when the Office would have been in some confusion.

[2] Thomas Witherings, in a pamphlet entitled *A Full and Cleare Answer to a False and Scandalous Paper, etc,* refers to Jude's service as "the first attempt that ever was made of carrying letters this way".

[3] Calendar State Papers, Domestic, 1619–23, pp. 238, 404.

[4] Journal, House of Commons, 1642–44, p. 477.

had a flair for administering the posts and was also keenly interested in the profits to be made out of them, for by now the Letter Office had become a lucrative one. Once its expenses were cleared, the remainder went to Prideaux. Also, like Witherings, he experienced much trouble and competition from "undertakers", as they were called, of private and unofficial posts. Prideaux had raised the rates for letter carrying, settling sixpence as the minimum, and extended the posts wherever he could. Most prominent of these "undertakers" were Clement Oxenbridge, who had at one time worked with Prideaux and had considerable experience in running the posts, and John Hill, an attorney of York. They were in partnership with others calling themselves "the first Undertakers for reducing letters to half the former rates". Not only did they effectively reduce the official postal rates to the former rates which had been fixed by Witherings but they also claimed to have speedier messengers. They showed that private enterprise could give a better service than an official monopoly, and the public responded by giving its support, so much so that Prideaux was compelled to reduce his rates by half. His repeated appeals to Parliament to protect his monopoly disclosed that the profits to be made from running a postal service were considerable, and worth far more than the £5,000 he was paying annually for it. The State therefore considered it should also be getting a bigger revenue and decided to let the Post Office "on farm" for a term of years, and tenders were invited.

Thus it came about that in 1653 the Post Office was farmed to Capt. John Manley, J.P., at a rental of £10,000 a year for a period of two years. Prideaux had become Solicitor-General in 1647, and Attorney-General a little later, a post which he retained until his death in 1659. It was probably the profits from the Post Office which had enabled him to purchase in 1649 a magnificent country estate in Somerset, Forde Abbey.

It was inevitable that such a state of affairs could not continue, with so many private undertakings competing with the government post. Therefore the Council of State issued a warrant:

> To Clement Oxenbridge, and all others concerned in the inland and foreign posts. *John Manley*, having contracted for and farmed these offices, we authorize him to enter on his duties this night (30.vi.53) to receive and carry all packets, and to receive all profits to his own

use. And you are required to permit him to do this without interruption or molestation.

The following year, after the expulsion of the Rump Parliament in 1653, an Ordinance was issued for the "Office of Postage of Letters, Inland and Foreign" which in very certain terms proclaimed this Office to be supreme in all matters relating to the carrying of letters; it was to be the only carrier of letters "in all the places of England, Scotland and Ireland and to and from all other places within the Dominions of the Commonwealth". An exception was made, however, for the country carriers with their wagons, and for servants carrying letters. Charges for letters were tabled with rules and regulations affecting the posts, who were to ride seven miles an hour during the summer months and five miles an hour the rest of the year. Postmasters were to keep at least four good horses for the post service, one always to be in readiness, and instructions were laid down for the foreign mail services and for the sailing of the packet boats to the Continent. From all of this, it can be seen how the Post Office was gradually developing and becoming established.

In 1655 the Secretary of State, John Thurloe, took over Manley's farm at the same rental. Two years later, in 1657, the Post Office was for the first time established by an Act of Parliament, with Thurloe as Postmaster General. This Act was more detailed than the previous Ordinance. It declared "there shall be one General Post Office and one officer styled the Postmaster General of England". Forbidden were "all other persons to set up or employ any footposts, horseposts or packet boats".

The undertakers were heard of again in 1659, when John Hill issued a pamphlet, *A PENNY POST: or, A Vindication of the Liberty and Birthright of every Englishman; in carrying Merchants and other men's Letters, against any restraint of Farmers of such Employments.* This pamphlet gives a long account of the injustice inflicted upon the people by the suppression of private enterprise on the part of the undertakers of postal services which were both quicker and cheaper than those the Government offered. It proposed, if given the authority to do so, to settle a post and carry letters anywhere in England for one penny, into Scotland for twopence, and into Ireland for fourpence.

With the restoration of the Monarchy in 1660 the new Government, not recognizing any laws passed during the Commonwealth,

A PENNY

POST:

OR, A

VINDICATION

OF THE

Liberty and Birthright

OF EVERY

ENGLISH-MAN;

IN

Carrying Merchants & other men's
Letters, againſt any reſtraint of Farmers of
ſuch Employments.

By *John Hill.*

LONDON,
Printed in the Yeare **1659.**

Fig. 3. *The title page of the rare eight-page pamphlet published by John Hill
in 1659. (Courtesy of the British Museum.)*

brought in a second Post Office Act[1] which virtually confirmed and repeated all that the previous Act had laid down. This Act has, in recent years, been referred to as the Post Office Charter.

The new Postmaster General was Colonel Henry Bishop, who had given active assistance to the Royalists during the King's absence abroad. He has now become known for having introduced the first date-stamp to be used on letters in April 1661. He was a Sussex gentleman who had for many years been an intimate friend of Major John Wildman—"the soul of English politics", to use Disraeli's description of him, and an absolute scamp. Wildman was deeply involved in many of the political plots which were a prominent feature of the seventeenth century. His ideas were Republican, and he was always plotting against whatever government was in power; giving help to whoever and whatever suited his purpose at the time. He skilfully wriggled out of many a tight corner, and always seemed to have the ability to get himself placed in some position with the Government, finally ending a notorious career as Postmaster General. It was probably Wildman who helped provide Bishop with the £21,500 now required yearly for the farm of the Post Office. In this way, and with his friend Bishop in nominal charge, Wildman could manipulate certain things within the Post Office without directing attention to himself. He was in fact in charge of an office "for the survey and inspection of letters", which was nothing more nor less than an office for collecting intelligence by intercepting the mail, nearly all of which was made to pass at some stage through the London office. Although nothing was directly traced to Wildman, there can be but little doubt that much of the meddling with the mail that went on in the Post Office was due to him. There is no doubt that this had been one of the activities of the Post Office ever since its earliest days.

In 1661, political tension running very high, there was suddenly trouble within the Post Office, and Henry Bishop had to answer for certain abuses charged against it, and some of his officials; among other things was the complaint of serious delay in the mail, which was due to the interception of letters. Subsequently an inquiry was held when, in his defence, Bishop wrote a statement in which he said "a stamp is invented that is putt upon every letter showing

---

[1] 12 Car. II, cap. 35.

the day of the moneth that every letter comes to the office, so that no Letter Carryer may dare to detayne a letter from post to post, which before was usual". This is one of the earliest references to the postmarking of letters in England.[1]

As a result of this inquiry, it was decided that no blame was attached to Bishop. His friend Wildman, however, was more deeply in trouble and was sent to prison accused of plotting against the Crown. Bishop relinquished his office of Postmaster General two years later, with several indictments against him. The Attorney-General, however, was ordered to halt the proceedings, probably on account of Bishop's loyalty to his Monarch. After which we hear nothing more of Bishop, who retired to his home in Henfield, in Sussex.

Not long after this, in 1663, a most unfortunate development took place. Parliament agreed to grant the profits from the Post Office to the King's brother, the Duke of York. A certain sum from the profits was reserved for the King himself, from which, after making sundry payments, he provided generous pensions to two of the Court favourites. This decision became a most serious one for the Post Office revenue, for it caused a most unnecessary drain on its income, from which it was never able to recover, and served to impede its development for many years to come. It is interesting, though possibly disturbing, to know that one of the pensions granted to a Court favourite that had descended to the Dukes of Grafton was rescinded only as recently as 1856, when it was commuted into a lump sum of £91,000!

---

[1] Sometimes erroneously described as the first postmark. Letters were marked by means of small handstamps in several of the Italian States and the Republic of Venice early in the fifteenth century. These were small uninked circular marks impressed on to the addressed side of letters, and usually showed the emblem or device of the town of origin. They were the forerunners of all postmarks.

CHAPTER 2

The London Penny Post

ROBERT MURRAY AND WILLIAM DOCKWRA—A PENNY POST
ESTABLISHED IN 1680—SUPPRESSED BY THE GOVERNMENT IN
1682—THE GOVERNMENT PENNY POST

WITH THE RESTORATION, there soon developed a remarkable increase in the desire for news, and an eagerness on the part of the public to express their opinions and spread them in such a manner as to bring pressure on the Government. Coffee houses, where news was exchanged and business discussed, soon began to spring up all over London. It was one of the duties of the Secretaries of State to see that the government monopoly of news, whether in print or manuscript, was officially licensed; otherwise it was assumed it would be false.

By 1680 the number of unofficial newspapers (or news-sheets) had increased considerably, and Whig newspapers in particular were being suppressed. The position with regard to unofficial news had become particularly acute as a result of the Popish Plot. Manuscript copies of proceedings in Parliament, in considerable numbers, were being circulated by hand, and were often of doubtful authenticity. Meanwhile news and official propaganda could be circulated by the Post Office throughout the country by means of subscriptions. It can readily be understood, therefore, how very useful a local postal system would be, whereby news-sheets, as well as letters, could be collected and delivered, in order to circumvent the controls. Just such a system was now being planned and was about to be organized.

London in the year 1680 was a very busy city. Much of the damage caused by the Great Fire in 1666 had been repaired and the old city was largely rebuilt. There had been no street planning—although Wren, Evelyn, and others had put forward plans—so that streets remained just where they had always been, narrow and

34

twisting, with a confusion of shop signs, many of them extremely elegant and beautiful. There was no street or house numbering, so that in order to direct to an address, it was quite usual to state at what sign in the street a person lived. This, too, was not always sufficient, so that when addressing a letter a directive would be written after the name explaining that he or she lived near to some tavern or some other building well known in the vicinity (see Plate 2b). A typical address shows on a letter dated 1682:

> This
> To Mr. Peter Le Neve att his house
> in east Hardon Street att the
> end of Gunpowder Alley from
> Shoe Lane over against the Door
> In the middle of the Dead Wall
> London.

The historian De Laune, writing in 1681, tells us that since the conflagration London had five hundred streets with a greatly increased number of houses; that rebuilding had greatly beautified the city, so that London "for fair and stately Edifices, uniform and Regular buildings and other publick Structures does not only excel its former State, but (all things considered) may outvie the most magnificent Cities of the Universe".

The General Post Office was now situated in Lombard Street, and was the residence of the Postmaster General and the principal officers. In the basement was a large office for the London letter carriers, of whom there were thirty-two. These carriers only delivered incoming letters to houses addressed throughout the city and suburbs. Several small shopkeepers in different parts of the City and in Westminster were licensed by the Post Office to receive letters. They were allowed to charge one penny a letter for the service of receiving and taking a letter to the General Post Office, or Head Office, as it was commonly called. A notice of 1652 lists names and addresses of twenty-one of these letter receivers, and refers to the Old Post House at the lower end of Threadneedle Street, which would not only be a letter office but also a place where horses could be hired and from whence some of the post-boys set forth on their journeys. Samuel Pepys mentions going to such a Post House, probably in order to hire a horse, not for the purpose of sending away a letter.

ALL Gentlemen Merchants, and other Perfons may pleafe to take notice, that upon Tuſeday night the eighteenth day of *January* 1652. the Letters were ſent from the old Poſt-houſe (at the lower end of Threedneedle-ſtreet, by the Stocks, in *London*) at the Rates of × twopence the ſingle Letter within eighty miles of *London*, and threepence the ſingle Letter above eighty miles within this Common-wealth (uſually ſent unto) and ſo proportionably for double Letters and Packets, and Packets of printed Books, or two ſhillings the pound, and the State Packets and Letters carried free : And ſo to continue going forth Tuſedays and Saturday nights, and Anſwers expected Mundays and Fryday mornings, as formerly accuſtomed.

And Letters may be received in for conveyance by
the old Poſt at thoſe Rates at the ſeveral places
accuſtomed. *V I Z.*

At Mr. *Bartholmew Haggets*, at the Sarizans Head in *Weſtminſter*.
At Mr. *Robert Genns*, the Roſe in King-ſtreet.
At Mr. *Edward Huchins*, Poſt-maſter, at the white hart at Charing Croſs
At Mr. *Adams*, the Porter of the Gate at the Savoy.
At Mr. *Ralph Oldhams*, at the Gun in the Strand.
At Mr. *William Leakes*, at the Crown at Temple Bar.
At Mr. *Lawrance Blacklocks*, at Temple Bar, Stationer.
At Mr. *Abell Ropers*, over againſt Dunſtones Church in Fleet-ſtreet.
At Mr. *Charles Adams*, the Marygold againſt Fetter lane end.
At Mr. *John Allins*, the white Horſe in Fleet-ſtreet.
At Mr. *Thomas Taylor*, in the inner Temple lane.
At Mr. *Lawrances*.
At *Matthew Days*, a Porter belonging to Lyons Inn.
At Mr. *Richard Beſt* Stationer in Graiſe-Inn Gate.
At Mr. *William Atkins*, Stationer at ſtaple Inn.
At Mr. *John Places*, Stationer at Furnifalls Inn.
At Mr. *Thomas Simms*, at the ſign of the Angel at Riddriff ſtayers.
At Capt. *Grigſons* next the white Lyon, by the new ſtayers at *Wapping*.
At Mrs. *Staltinborgh*, Tower-hill next the Navy Office.
At Mrs. *Smith* next the Cock in *Ratlef*.
At Mrs. *Ivy* over againſt the Gun in Woodſtreet.

*The Perſons that leave Letters at any of theſe places, are deſired to bring
them in thither before ten of the clock, Tuſedays and Saturday nights;
and at the Poſt-houſe by the Stocks by twelve a clock.*

Fig. 4. *A little-known notice of 1652 listing the Letter Receivers of the City of London.* (*Courtesy the Guildhall Library, London.*)

As well as the licensed letter receivers there were many taverns and coffee houses which were commonly used as accommodation addresses or "postes restante". The coffee houses in particular were to become closely associated with the Post Office for a number of years, especially with regard to overseas mail. They were places where people met to discuss business and were the rendezvous of sea captains and merchants, where arrivals and departures of ships could be advertised. A bag was placed somewhere handy for the reception of letters, and a penny, sometimes twopence, for each letter would be left for the captain as his gratuity for taking it.

Although London had grown quite considerably to a population of about half a million, it was strange that the Post Office provided no service for the collection and delivery of local letters and parcels. In order to send a letter from one part of London to another, it was usual to send it either by a servant or by means of a hired porter or messenger. To Kent and the Downs there was a post daily, also a daily Essex post; to other parts of England and to Scotland a post went every other day; and to Wales and to Ireland a post went every week. England itself was served by six main post-roads, namely Chester, West, Bristol, North, Yarmouth, and Kent. Several of the main Post Towns on these roads had bye-posts, which dealt with letters from some of the larger towns off the main routes. The system was fairly simple and brought most of the country letters into or through London. But it did not cater for local London letters.

There must have been considerable surprise, then, when Londoners read, on March 22, 1680, a small notice in the columns of a new Whig newspaper *Mercurius Civicus*:

> We are informed some ingenious persons and good Citizens, for the benefit of the City and Suburbs in point of charge and quick conveyance of Notes and Letters, have projected a method for doing the same throughout for 1d. a Letter one with another, further or nearer, which may be termed a Foot-Post, whereof our next may give you more particular account.

Two days later the next issue announced:

> The Project and Carriage of Town Letters which we mentioned in our last, is as we hear of great charge to the undertakers, and can consequently be of prejudice to none but themselves, since the Publick use is visible to all who know the difference one penny a Letter and the

37

Price they now pay. And it is heartily to be wisht that their Zeal to the publick has not put them upon wrong computations to their future discouragement, that being the common Fate of most Ingenious designs.

These are the earliest announcements of what was to be London's first Penny Post, and because they appeared in a new Whig newspaper at a time when public opinion was still very much shaken by the recent disclosure of the Popish Plot by the notorious Titus Oates, the scheme was associated by both Whigs and Catholics with being an instrument of political design.

Newspapers were quick to challenge and attack the new project, mainly on grounds that it was believed to be connected with the Catholic cause, though one paper reported that it would "no more serve the Papists to plot, than the Protestants to counterplot them, the advantage being equal". Other papers wrote of the resentment shown by the porters, who feared they would be out of work through having no letters or parcels to carry, and described how they were pulling down the placards which advertised the scheme from outside the receiving houses. *Mercurius Civicus* reported on April 27 how two porters were brought before the bench and fined for "Tareing down a label" from a Penny Post receiving house in Wick Street near St. Clement's Church, the Court "taking notice of their rude Language as well as their Breach of the Peace".

One of the more aggressive newspapers was *Smith's Current Intelligence* run by a Nonconformist bookseller, which favoured neither Whigs nor Catholics. Smith's comments were so virulent that the Whigs prosecuted him for his criticism of the Penny Post, and he was suspended for a while.

So it was that this wonderful project was conceived and introduced to the citizens of London in a confusion of political unrest and intrigue, typical of those days.

The two originators of the scheme were both Londoners, Robert Murray and William Dockwra. Robert Murray was born in the Strand in 1633 and had been in and out of many occupations before meeting Dockwra; he seems to have been a man with a mind for making money quickly, turning from one job to another, and gifted in being able to produce ingenious ideas. William Dockwra was born in London in 1635, in Coleman Street not far from the Church of St. Olave Jewry. In his early twenties, under the patronage of the Earl of Southampton, he was given a position as a Customs under-searcher in the Port of London and paid a salary of £12 a year. A Treasury warrant of January 22, 1663/4 made out by the Earl of Southampton, Lord High Treasurer of England, did

> give and grant unto Willm. Docwra of London, Gent. the office or place of Under Searcher or subsearcher in the said Port of London upon the surrender of John Norwood, Gent. to have hold and enjoy the said office of undersearcher . . . during his Majesty's pleasure, to-gether with all such fees, profits, advantages & commodities, as usually are.

The perquisites that went with the office are mentioned by De Laune in his *Present State of London*, "there were sundry Fees setled upon them (the sub-searchers) by Authority of Parliament which are paid them by Masters of Ships, and Merchants". For a young man of those days Dockwra was unquestionably holding quite a good position, but after only ten years in 1673/4 he left it, which rather indicates that he was planning to enter into something more profitable.

In the 1670s Dockwra is known to have been owner of a sailing ship, the *Anne*, which traded along the Guinea coast, for some twenty years later, in 1696, he recovered from the Royal Africa Company of England the sum of £2,000 (a very considerable amount of money in those days) as a result of the *Anne* being seized by a man-of-war, accused of encroaching upon the rights of the Company. For a man of those days he can be considered as well-to-do, and was certainly never poor. How he came to meet Robert Murray, his partner in the Penny Post scheme, is not known. Doubtless it was Murray who discussed the possibilities of a Penny Post with Dockwra, which, according to No. 77 of *The True Domestic Intelligence* of March 1680, took place some time during 1678. Dockwra must have been greatly impressed with the idea, for he invested almost all, if not the whole, of his money in the scheme.[1]

There has always been dispute as to which one of them was the actual inventor of the Penny Post; Murray claims he was both inventor and first proposer of it, and says so on a small trade-card which he published, which is now in the British Museum; un-

[1] The idea was not a novel one, for a local Penny Post had been tried in Paris in 1653—see Appendix I, p. 153.

fortunately it is not dated. Dockwra, on the other hand, whose name has always been connected with the Penny Post, called himself the "Author" of it. What we know to have happened is that the partnership did not last for very long, for soon after they started Murray was involved in some political trouble and was arrested, causing the partnership to break-up and leaving Dockwra to carry on alone. Murray is never again heard of working with Dockwra, but both of them in later years exchanged very angry letters and published statements denying the other's claim as

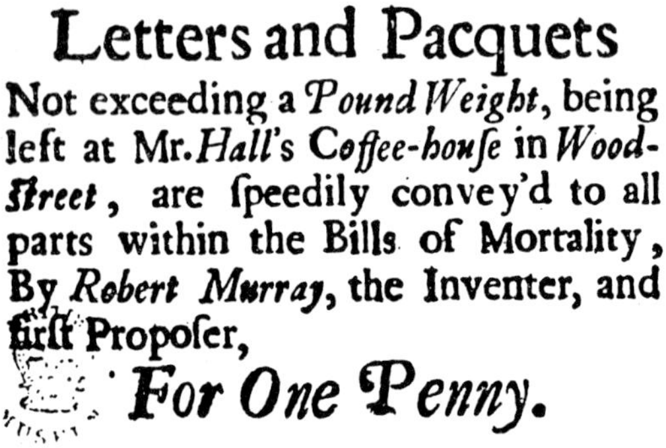

Letters and Pacquets

Not exceeding a *Pound Weight*, being left at Mr. *Hall's Coffee-house* in *Wood-Street*, are speedily convey'd to all parts within the Bills of Mortality, By *Robert Murray*, the Inventer, and first Propofer,

For One Penny.

Fig. 5. *This undated "trade-card" is in the British Museum (Harleian MSS. Bagford Collection 5954). It confirms Robert Murray's claim to be the inventor of the Penny Post.*

original inventor of the Penny Post.[1]

Among the many projects Murray had dabbled in was one connected with banking; this is described in the *Dictionary of National Biography* as "a proposal for a combined bank and Lombard or *mont de pieté* for the issue of credit against dead stock deposited at 6 per cent interest". In one of these banking projects he undoubtedly made the acquaintance of an interesting character named Dr. Hugh Chamberlen (sometimes spelt Chamberlain) described as "a physicist and economist". This gentleman had become known in 1666 through his plan for freeing London from the plague. He was a man of questionable character, but a good friend of Murray's. He came into the Penny Post project, offering his services in an advisory capacity. He is often referred to as one of the "undertakers" of the scheme, but he himself publicly denied this in an issue of the *London Gazette* for May 1680. He was a man who was sometimes involved in dubious practices, and was often entangled in the political troubles of those times. As a doctor he won fame for being a male midwife. On one occasion, however, he was fined £10—

[1] See Appendix II, p. 157.

with the alternative of being gaoled in Newgate—for the "illegal and evil practice of medicine". But he was certainly a very able man and managed to remain in the Royal favour, for he attended Mary of Modena in her confinements and became Physician-in-ordinary to Charles II in 1673. In 1681 he was elected a Fellow of the Royal Society. As was the case with many prominent people of those days, he was implicated in politics, and, being a Whig, was made to suffer for his principles when the Whig Government fell from power in 1682. He came into prominence again in 1690 when he was occupied with his Land Bank, which was to make England "Rich and Happy", and in 1702 he was the author of what has been described as "one of the ablest pamphlets ever written on behalf of a political cause", when he supported the proposed union of Scotland and England. Some years afterwards he went to Holland, and after 1720 nothing more is known of him.

The only other of the known undertakers in the scheme was a Mr. Henry Neville Payne, frequently referred to as Henry Nevil. Neville Payne was mentioned in *Smith's Current Intelligence* in connection with the Popish Plot, when Oates referred to the Penny Post as the "dexterous invention" of Nevil. The *Dictionary of National Biography* describes him as a "conspirator and author". He was arrested in December 1678 because of his activities at the time of the Popish Plot. Neville Payne seems to have been a shady and unpleasant character who was implicated on several occasions in political matters, and was often in and out of prison. His name is also remembered for having been the last person to suffer torture in Scotland, in 1690, and as late as December 1700 he was known to be in prison.

A complete picture of the organization of the Penny Post is contained in a most interesting little historical guide book already referred to, *The Present State of London*, by Thos. De Laune, published in 1681.[1] From this very detailed account we know that the Head Office was in Lime Street in the house formerly lived in by Sir Robert Abdy. There were seven sorting houses established at more or less equal distances serving the cities of London and Westminster and the Suburbs.

There are about 4–500 Receiving-houses to take in Letters, where the Messengers call every hour, and convey them as directed; as also

[1] See Appendix III, p. 160.

Post-Letters, the writing of which are much increased by the Accommodation being carefully convey'd by them to the General Post Office in Lombard Street.

Employment was given to "a great number of Clerks and poor Citizens . . . as Messengers to collect, Sort, Enter, stamp and deliver all Letters". Letters and parcels not exceeding one pound in weight and £10 in value were collected and delivered on pre-payment of one penny, which charge also included insurance. In one of Dockwra's broadsides, entitled *The Practical Method of the Penny Post*, the undertakers declared themselves not responsible for any "Breaking, Damage of Choice and Curious Things; nor Glasses or Liquid Matter sent by them, it being altogether unreasonable . . ." It explained further that the contents or the value should be plainly written on the outside of the packages "forasmuch, as there has been sundry attempts to cheat the Undertakers of many pounds, by false Endorsements of Money, and pretences of Loss of other things sent in small Parcels, which really never were sent at all, an ungrateful return for the Undertakers kindness . . .".

An important novelty for those days was the use of postmarks showing the time of day letters had been stamped as they passed through the office. As already mentioned, the first date-stamp was introduced by Henry Bishop in 1661. This showed a simple abbreviated date within a very small circle. Dockwra now employed small heart-shaped stamps with MOR for morning service and AF for afternoon service followed by a figure which signified the hour of the day (see Plate 2a). A triangular stamp inscribed PENNY POST PAID was applied to letters and showed the initial letter of one of the seven sorting houses and that of the Head Office in Lime Street. These postmarks ensured a check on letter carriers so that should a letter not be delivered within little more than an hour from the time shown in the heart-shaped postmark the recipient was encouraged to complain.

These Penny Post Paid handstamps were an innovation for those days. They were, in fact, the first Paid stamps ever to be used in the world.

The opening date of the Penny Post is reported in *Smith's Current Intelligence* for March 27, 1680:

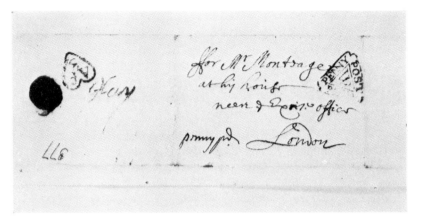

Plate 2a. A Dockwra-stamped letter dated July 18, 1681. The receiver's name Hay is seen near to the heart-shaped time stamp. The triangular Penny stamp shows the W of the Westminster office.

Plate 2b. A letter dated February 4, 1683 showing a typical address in the City of London.

YORK and LEEDS
Broad-Wheel Stage-Waggons,

SET out from the GEORGE and WHITE HART Inn in *Aldersgate-Street, London,* every Monday about Two of the Clock in the Afternoon, and will be at *Doncaster* on *Saturday,* and at the *White Swan* on the Pavement *York* on *Tuesday* following at Eleven o' Clock, and carry Goods and Passengers to and from LONDON, YORK, LEEDS, SCARBOROUGH, HULL, BEVERLEY, KNARESBRO', RIPPON, STOCKTON, STOKESLEY, BE-DELL, DARLINGTON, NORTHALERTON, GISBROROUGH, MALTON, HOW-DEN, YARM, PONTEFRACT, DONCASTER, BARNSLEY, THORNE, RETFORD, NEWARK, GRANTHAM, and all other Places on that Road on the most reasonable Terms.

Performed, if God permit, by
{ Thomas Pheazant,
Francis Smith,
Francis Haworth,
Thomas Hawksworth, } Of *Doncaster.*

AND

William Massey, in the *Strand, London.*

☞ A Waggon sets out from *Leeds* every *Saturday* for *Doncaster,* and returns to *Leeds* every *Monday.* Also another Waggon sets out from *Barnsley* to *Doncaster* every *Saturday,* and returns the same Day to *Barnsley,* and is the only Carriage that goes to *Barnsley.*

N. B. Passengers to *York* Ten Shillings; to *Doncaster* Eight Shillings each; and so in Proportion for any other Part of the Road.

Post Boy

Plate 3*a* (*above*). A mid-eighteenth-century Carrier's notice.

Plate 3*b*. A post-boy, late eighteenth century.

On Saturday Last The Projectors for Conveying Letters to any part of the City, or Suburbs, for a penny a Letter, opened their offices, whereof the three chiefest are in Lime Street, about Charing-Cross and Temple-bar; besides several inferior Offices; at which they have hung out tables to advertise people of the thing.

Fig. 6. *Dockwra's Penny Post stamps 1680–82.*

An advertisement in *Mercurius Civicus* on April 6 announced:

The Undertakers for the Incomparable and Advantagious Design for the Speedy and Safe Conveyance of Letters and Packquets under a pound weight, to all parts of the Cities of London and Westminster, and the Suburbs thereof, finding that their Houses appointed for the Receit of such Letters are not as yet fully completed, have for the present and further accommodation of all persons therein, ordered their Messengers to call for all Letters at all Coffee-Houses in the High Roads and Streets following, every hour in some places and an hour and a half in the rest, viz:—

From Westminster through the Strand and St. Paul's Church-yard, through Cheapside and Cornhil to Aldgate. From Ratcliff-cross through the Highway to Little-Tower-Hill. And from Ratcliff-cross the Lower way through Shadwell and Wapping to the Hermitage, and so through St. Katherines to the Iron-gate. From St. Georges Church in South-wart to London-Bridge; Then from the Bridge, through Grace-Church street to Shoreditch Church. Also from St. Giles's through Holborn to the Entrance of Cheapside And lastly in Chancery-Lane.

And all persons, who leave their Letters at any of the places aforesaid, may be sure to have them speedily dispatch'd for

ONE PENY

And the Undertakers do intend, in a few days, to settle many more places of Receit for the accommodation of other parts of both Cities and Suburbs.

This indicates that Dockwra and his partners experienced difficulty at the outset in providing as many receiving houses as they had

43

intended. The organization of so vast a scheme as this would have required an enormous amount of planning, quite apart from substantial financial backing. It seems to suggest also that the scheme was being started before it was ready. It is quite likely they had powerful Whig support, and that the Whigs wanted the project to start quickly to help in the distribution of Whig propaganda.

A serious set-back was encountered later in the year when the project was challenged by the Duke of York on the grounds that it infringed his monopoly by the Act of Charles II which established one General Post Office, and, as a consequence, several actions were brought against Dockwra. Thanks to the Whig Government under the powerful Earl of Shaftesbury, which had always shown itself sympathetic to the Penny Post, the Whig Judges gave a verdict in Dockwra's favour, and he was able to carry on. It is apparent that the undertakers of the Penny Post had many friends in the Whig Government, and must have had someone with considerable influence at Court to help them, presumably the Earl of Shaftesbury. As Thomas De Laune says:

> questionless, the Duke is better inform'd now; for it is most certain that this does much further the Revenue of the Grand Post-Office, and is an universal Benefit to all the Inhabitants of these Parts: so that whoever goes about to deprive the City of so useful a thing, deserves no thanks from the Duke, nor any Body else, but to be Noted as an *Enemy* to *Publick and Ingenious Inventions.*

As well as the publicity given to the Penny Post in the several newspapers, a good account of it is found in the many notices and handbills which Dockwra published,[1] the earliest and best known being the one entitled "A Penny Well Bestowed", which appeared in April of 1680. This broadside described the many advantages offered by the "new design" and advertised all the places to be served "within the Cities and Suburbs of London and Westminster . . . and the Out Parishes within the Weekly Bills of Mortality", meaning the parishes in and around London which gave a periodic return of deaths. In summer letters would be delivered from six in the morning until nine at night "and at reasonable hours agreeable to the Winter Season". To the more distant parts of London letters

[1] Many of these are to be seen in the British Museum and the Guildhall Library.

1680.

A PENNY

Well Beſtowed,

Or a Brief Account of the *New Deſign* contrived for the great Increaſe of *Trade*, and Eaſe of *Correſpondence*, to the great Advantage of the Inhabitants of all ſorts, by Conveying of *LETTERS* or *PACQUETS* under a Pound Weight, to and from all parts within the Cities of *London* and *Weſtminſter*; and the Out Pariſhes within the *VVeekly Bills* of *Mortality*,

For One Penny.

 Here is nothing tends more to the increaſe of Trade and Buſineſs than a Speedy, Cheap, and ſafe way of *Intelligence*, much being obſtructed and more retarded in all Places where that is wanting. For as Money, like the Blood in Natural Bodies, gives Life to Trade by its Circulation; ſo Correſpondence like the Vital Spirits, gives it Senſe and Motion: and the more that theſe abound in any Place, the more doth that Place increaſe in Riches, Strength, and Vigor.

But in this Age it is not to be expected that any New Deſign can be contrived for the Publick Good, without meeting many raſh Cenſures and Impediments, from the Fooliſh and Malicious; therefore 'twas not likely this ſhould eſcape that common Fate. Yet We hope to all the reaſonable and Candid, who are willing to underſtand their own Intereſt, this Paper may be Satisfactory.

For 'tis undertaken by the Methods of that Correſpondency ſettled, that any Perſon may promiſe himſelf his *Letter* or *Pacquet* ſhall ſafely come to any place directed to, lying within the Cities and Suburbs of *London* and *VVeſtminſter*, and all their contiguous Buildings; alſo to *VVapping*, *Ratcliſſe*, *Lyme-houſe*, *Poplar* and *Blackwall*; to *Redriſſe*, *Southwark*, and ſo to *Newington* and *Lambeth*; to *Hackney*, *Iſlington*; and all other places within the *Weekly Bills* of *Mortality*, be it farther or nearer, to and from any of the aforeſaid Places,

For One Penny.

The times for iſſuing out of *Letters* to any of the aforeſaid Places, to be in the Summer time from Six in the Morning to Nine at Night, and at reaſonable hours agreeable to the Winter Seaſon.

To the moſt remote Places *Letters* ſhall be ſent at leaſt Five times a day.

To Places of quick Negotiation within the City, and in the Term time for ſervice of the Law Buſineſs, &c. at leaſt Fifteen times a day.

No *Letters* that come after Nine at Night, to be delivered till next Morning (except ſuch Letters as are for the *Poſt-Office* General.)

By this means all Perſons, as well Gentlemen, Lawyers, Shop-keepers, and Handicrafts Men, that make and deal in Commodities vended by Patterns and poor Priſoners, and all others, have that diſpatched for a *Penny*, which uſually coſts Three Pence, Six Pence, or a Shilling. Now to oblige Men to pay more when they can hereby be cheaper ſerved, were to impoſe an illegal Tax upon the Inhabitants without their Conſents.

Beſides many Journeys of Taylors, Weavers, and other poor Artificers, and their Servants, will be ſpared, who now conſume much time abroad in going to and fro, to the impoveriſhing of their Families, becauſe they cannot extravagantly pay a Porter for a Meſſage,

Fig. 7. *The front of the firſt broadſheet to be publiſhed by William Dockwra in April 1680. (Courteſy of the Guildhall Library, London.)*

would be sent at least five times a day, and "To Places of quick Negotiation within the City, and in Term time for service of the Law Business, &c, at least fifteen times a day". Letters coming in after nine at night (except those for the General Post Office) would be held over till the next morning.

Continuing in a picturesque choice of words, it goes on to say that:

> By this means all Persons, as well Gentlemen, Lawyers, Shop-keepers, and Handicrafts Men, that make and deal in Commodities vended by Patterns and Poor Prisoners, and all others, have that dispatched for a *Penny*, which usually costs Three Pence, Six Pence, or a Shilling. . . . Besides many Journeys of Taylors, Weavers, and other poor Artificers, and their Servants, will be spared, who now consume much time abroad in going to and fro, to the impoverishing of their Families, because they cannot extravagantly pay a Porter for a Message, or Carrying a Letter. But now their time will be imployed in their Callings at home, to the better Maintenance of their Charges.

After further explanation as to the benefits of the plan it concludes by listing "Some of the Conveniences of this Undertaking":

> All Countrey Gentlemen, Traders, &c, can hereby give notice to Friends of their Arrival to Town.
> Lawyers and Clyents correspond about necessary Occurences in Law.
> Much time is saved in Solicitation for Moneys.
> Easy notice given of all meetings between men of Business at a remote distance.
> Parents may Converse with their absent Children at Boarding-Schooles, &c.
> Children with their Parents to the Improvement of their Hands, Stile and Learning.
> Mathematick, Musick, Singing, Dancing-Masters and Teachers of Languages, to give notice of all disappointments to their Schollers.
> The sick Patients frequently to Correspond with their Doctors and Apothecaries.
> And many more profitable and pleasant uses may be made of this cheap way of Correspondence, too many to enumerate.
> Therefore we shall leave all the Ingenious to find out wherein our Invention may be servicable to them, and refer all people to be convinced by Time and Experience.
>
> THE TRUE TOUCHSTONE OF ALL DESIGNS

In spite of the attacks and criticisms made about the Penny Post on its inception, it soon proved all that it claimed to do, and its usefulness and popularity quickly eliminated any opposition there had been. Many of the discontented porters were absorbed into the

By the PENNY POST. *Lyme-ſtreet.*

THE Undertakers *having at a vaſt Charge engaged in a very difficult and hazardous* Deſign, *for the Accommodation of the City and parts adjacent, in the ſpeedy and ſafe conveyance of all Letters as well* Poſt Letters *to* Lombard Street, *as* Town Letters *to other places, for* One Penny *a Letter or Pacquet; and though ſome Lovers of* Ingenious *Deſigns for Publick Good, to encourage this, have willingly intruſted them with the Carriage of their* Poſt Letters *to the* Poſt Office General, *on Poſt Nights, yet ſome perſons through neglect of this uſeful Contrivance, have preferr'd the Bell-man and other obſcure perſons, rather than the uſe of the* Penny Poſt, *on whom they might more confidently rely, than on any other Conveyance whatſoever; they keeping an Exact Regiſtry of all* Poſt Letters, *atteſted under the hand of the Conveyer: whereby they are always ready to vouch the due Delivery thereof. And that ſeeing the Income ariſing from the Carriage of* Town Letters *doth not near anſwer the* Charge *the* Undertakers *are at, They do hope all* Ingenious Perſons *will for their future Encouragement, intruſt their Receiving Houſes with the Receipt of their* Poſt Letters Inland or Foreign; *whence they ſhall be carefully called for, till between the hours of* Nine *and* Ten *at Night, and ſafely conveyed to the* Poſt Office General,

For ONE PENNY a Letter or Pacquet.

And any perſon writing divers Letters, and putting them under one Cover, directed to the *Poſt Office General* in *Lombardſtreet*, the ſame ſhall be conveyed thither for *One Penny*; and for ſuch *Poſt Letters* as pay here, the Money is deſired to be Endorced on ſuch Letters.

London, Printed by *Tho. James* at the *Printing-preſs* in *Mincing-lane*. 1681.

Fig. 8. *One of the many handbills distributed by William Dockwra in 1681. It contains the earliest known reference to a bellman. (Courtesy The Trustees of the British Museum.)*

organization as messengers; some four to five hundred receiving houses from one end of London to the other, and in the suburbs as well, were available for taking in letters, so that London, which had never had a local post of its own, was now in possession of one which has never since been equalled.

It had been in operation for nearly two years, and Dockwra and his partners might have confidently expected a just reward for all their efforts, with receipts just beginning to exceed expenses. The undertaking was beginning to prosper and showed every sign of being a certain financial success when the Duke of York again complained that the undertaking was in violation of the monopoly of the Post Office, from which he received the profits.

The Postmaster General, the Earl of Arlington, proceeded against Dockwra, and this time, as there had been a change of government with the Whigs out of office and their leader the Earl of Shaftesbury fled to Holland, the action went against Dockwra. He was fined only £100 for contempt of court, but he lost his Penny Post, which was wrested from him and incorporated into the General Post Office.

Fig. 9. *Types of London Penny Post stamps, 1689–1707.*

The Government was now in possession of an excellent well-organized business, and forthwith, only a few days after the judgement, announced in the *London Gazette* that the Penny Post would shortly be re-opened. It re-opened on December 11, 1682, as a completely separate office from the General Post Office, and was controlled and run on very similar lines to those which Dockwra had employed. With only slight variations, the same sort of stamps were used, the day of the week being added to the triangular stamps. The head office of the Penny Post was now transferred from Lime Street to Crosby House in Bishopsgate and again later to St. Christopher's Alley in Threadneedle Street.

Dockwra now lost no time in appealing for compensation for the loss he had suffered and petitioned the Duke of York for the farm of the Penny Post, explaining he had lost almost all his money in the venture, and made an impassioned plea that the farm of the Penny Post would save him and his wife and eight children from ruin. But the Duke of York (later King James II) was not a person noted for his generosity, and the Petition was turned down. For many years William Dockwra persisted in his petitions and pleas for a reward and compensation in recognition of all he had done in organizing the Penny Post, which by now had become an institution.

Many of these petitions are to be seen today in the Public Records Office, and they certainly give the impression that Dockwra was a ruined man. But although he had suffered a set-back in his fortunes, he was never actually a poor man in the accepted meaning of the word. Eventually, by the grace of King William III in 1691, he was given a pension of £500 a year to run for seven years, which was to be paid out of the profits of the Penny Post. This was later extended for another three years. In 1692 he is heard of in partnership with a Mr. John Green of Carteret Street "by the Cock-pit Royal" busy with another idea of his. The *Athenian Mercury* for April 9, 1692, carries an advertisement headed "William Dockwra's Easie Coaches". This was a patent of Dockwra's, the coaches being "hung so to render them easier for the Passenger, and less labour to the Horses . . . the Coachmen's sitting more convenient and the motion just like that of a Sedan being free from that tossing and joulting to which other Coaches are liable". The notice carried the hope of Dockwra that this invention would fare better than his one for the Penny Post!

Shortly afterwards Dockwra is heard of in America, and is recorded in the *American Dictionary of National Biography* in association with Andrew Hamilton, the appointed deputy to Thomas Neale, who held a Royal patent to establish and operate the posts in North America. The reference says briefly, "Hamilton's interest may have been due to his relations with William Dockwra, an East Jersey proprietor, who had established a penny post in London". It is, however, almost certain that Dockwra was never in America, but, as was common in those days, he was probably represented over there by proxy. He was associated with the Board of Proprietors of the Eastern Division of New Jersey (the Board is still in existence today) as Secretary and Registrar, and owned, at the time of his death, one-twelfth of the State. In connection with this project, Dockwra acted as proxy for the Earl of Perth, which indicates that Dockwra was indeed a man of substance, and of good social position.

In 1693 Dockwra was busy in partnership with others for another

49

"invention" and applied for a grant of Letter Patent for an incorporated company to be known by the name of "The Governor and Company for Casting and Making Guns and Ordnance in Moulds of Metal". He had already been elected Master of the Armourer's Company—a very important position in London in those days—and was an unsuccessful candidate as Chamberlain of the City of London in 1695.

In 1696 Dockwra was once again in the Penny Post Office with the position of Comptroller of that office. But he had now become an irritable man and difficult to get along with, and his management was vastly different from what it had been when he first set up his own Penny Post. In consequence of many complaints made against him, he was dismissed in 1700, after a very fair and adequate hearing. The complaints stated that:

> Hee hath removed the general Penny-post from Cornhill, a place most proper, being near the 'Change, and in the heart of the citty, to a more remote place altogether improper, whereby the messengers' walks are altered from one to two houres, so that letters are thereby delayed for some hours, to the great hindrance of business and fatigue to the poor messengers, and £100 charges to His Majesty to fit his house for his own convenience. Hee forbids the taking in any bandboxes (except very small), and all parcels above a pound, which, when they were taken, did bring in considerable advantage to the office, they being now at great charge sent by porters in the citty, and coaches and water men into the country, which formerly went by Penny-post messengers much cheaper and more satisfactorily. Hee stops, under spetious pretences, most parcells that are taken in, which is great damage to tradesmen by losing their customers or spoiling their goods, and many times hazard the life of the patient, when physick is sent by a doctor or an apothecary.

Dockwra at once began petitioning for redress, airing all his old pleas. He re-affirmed his claim to be the inventor of the Penny Post, and published angry announcements in the Press denying the claim of Murray to have been the originator.

Murray was never mentioned again working with Dockwra after their partnership was broken. In September 1681 he was given employment as an agent of the Earl of Shaftesbury, and was heard of in Paris. From time to time he tried his hand at several unusual occupations, but does not appear to have been very successful, for he was often in debt. Dockwra mentions giving him a loan on one occasion and says, "I often bayl'd him to keep him out of prison." He is last heard of as controller and paymaster of the National Lottery, having had dealings with the South Sea Company in 1721.

William Dockwra died in 1716 in the City of London, and was buried in the Church of St. Olave Jewry, long since pulled down. His death was recorded in a number of papers and journals, very few agreeing on his age, some stating that he was near a hundred. Most of them gave him the credit for having been the inventor of the Penny Post.

The Government managed the Penny Post on much the same lines as it had been originally planned, with only slight changes. At first there had been seven principal offices, now there were six, the chief one being in Cornhill. The others were St. Paul's, Queen's Head Alley in Newgate Street; the Temple office, Chichester Rents in Chancery Lane; the Westminster office in St. Martin's Lane near Charing Cross; the Southwark office near St. Mary Overy's Church, and the Hermitage office in Swedeland Court by East Smithfield.

CHAPTER 3

A Century of Development

CHARLES POVEY'S "HALF-PENNY CARRIAGE"—THE ACT OF 1711
—RALPH ALLEN—THE ACT OF 1765—PETER WILLIAMSON—
—THE EDINBURGH PENNY POST—JOHN PALMER AND THE MAIL-
COACH SYSTEM—PROVINCIAL PENNY POSTS—REORGANIZATION
OF THE LONDON PENNY POST IN 1794—A PENNY POST FOR
SOLDIERS AND SAILORS

WHEN WILLIAM OF ORANGE landed at Brixham on November 5, 1688, there were many with him who were returning to England from exile, having seen fit to leave England during the difficult years of James II's reign. Among them was Major John Wildman, who, as we have seen, was an associate of Colonel Bishop, Postmaster General after the Restoration. Wildman had fled the country after being implicated in the Monmouth rebellion, and was lucky in getting out of the country and into Holland. In The Hague he became a central figure among the supporters of William of Orange. A contemporary reference to him says, "Among the English who came to The Hague was one Wildman, who, from being an agitator in Cromwell's army, had been a constant meddler on all occasions in everything that looked like sedition."

Now that he was back in England he was to be rewarded for his services and loyalty to William. He was offered the valuable post of Lieutenant of the Ordnance, but refused it. Instead, he had James II's Postmaster General, Philip Frowde, removed from office and took his place.

With the new Government and a new sovereign there were many rewards and favours to be bestowed on all sorts of individuals who had been "badly done by" one way or another during the successive governments of the past ten to fifteen years. Clement Oxenbridge was remembered for the part he took by getting postal rates reduced during the Prideaux administration, and William Dockwra, "in consideration of his good service in inventing and setting up the business of the Penny Post Office", received a £500 a year pension mentioned earlier.

Although Wildman proved a capable and useful Postmaster General, responsible for several improvements (it was his idea to establish Falmouth as a Post Office Packet port), he did not remain long in that office, for he was unable to keep out of political intrigue, and was suspected of tampering with correspondence in the Foreign Branch of the Post Office. King William, however, seemed well disposed towards him and bestowed the honour of a knighthood on him shortly before Wildman's death in 1693. He was the last Postmaster General to hold that office alone for some while, for after his dismissal in 1691 the office was put into commission, being held jointly until 1823. The new Postmasters General were Sir Robert Cotton and Sir Thomas Frankland, two very conscientious administrators who carefully directed the policies of the Post Office through very difficult times.

On October 4, 1709, a surprising individual, by name Charles Povey, impudently challenged the Post Office monopoly by starting a privately run enterprise which he called the "Half-Penny Carriage". It was modelled on very similar lines to the Penny Post of Dockwra, except it was confined to the busy parts of London and Westminster and to the borough of Southwark. Receiving houses were set up in shops and small businesses, and for the price of one halfpenny Povey undertook to collect and deliver letters and packages. He popularized the use of bellmen by having messengers patrol the streets every hour ringing a bell so that people, on hearing, could be waiting with their letters and spared the trouble of going to one of the receiving houses. Doubtless the idea was intended by way of advertisement, but people quickly appreciated its convenience, and his undertaking was popular and successful. Naturally it was quickly suppressed by the Crown. Povey's Half-Penny Carriage lasted exactly seven months, when proceedings were taken against him and he was fined £100, along with several of his bell-ringers and shopkeepers who, having acted as receivers, were fined for their part in the venture. The idea of bell-ringers for collecting

53

letters in the streets was considered a useful one by the Post Office, and this was the one permanent result of Povey's venture, for henceforth bellmen collected letters in the streets of London until 1846. The practice was adopted in other towns too, Dublin being the last city to give it up in 1859, although it lingered in the country for some years.[1]

In keeping with his character, Povey displayed an extraordinary attitude towards the authorities, almost daring them to stop him in his project, and he continued his protests for long after his conviction. Povey was a remarkable man in many ways. In the same year that he began his Half-Penny Carriage he founded a fire-insurance company, which became the Sun Fire Office. In a short history of their house this famous insurance company have described Povey as being a man of enormous ingenuity of invention; an author, inventor, politician, a projector of public companies, and a public benefactor. But he showed a quick temper to anyone who opposed him, and made many enemies. A contemporary refers to him as "a cantankerous character, a very great religious professor, and yet always in 'hot water' with some one". He was his own enemy. Fortunately for himself he was never actually a poor man, for he states in one of his writings that "A Divine Providence sent me, from an unforeseen Quarter, a plentiful fortune, to enable me to lend to the Poor . . .", and when he died in 1743 his will bore testimony to his benevolence.

This episode of Povey's Half-Penny Carriage happened at a time when the Crown was considering new legislation for the Post Office. Since Queen Anne came to the throne in 1702 the country had been involved in the War of the Spanish Succession. The Post Office, which already provided large funds for many pensions and grants, was now to be mulcted for the heavy debts incurred by war.

When the new Post Office Act was proclaimed in 1711[2] it was entitled "An Act for establishing a General Post Office for all Her Majesty's Dominions, and for settling a Weekly Sum out of the Revenues thereof, for the service of the War, and other Her Majesty's Occasions". It required the Post Office to pay £700 weekly into the Exchequer. All postal rates were raised, except the London Penny Post, which for the first time was given Parliamentary sanction. The

[1] See Appendix IV, p. 168, and Plate 4.
[2] 9 Anne, cap. 10.

Act forbade anyone to collect letters in the City of London or its suburbs except under licence by the Postmasters General under penalty of heavy fines—a direct result of Charles Povey's audacious enterprise. An important change made concerning the Penny Post was to limit its scope to within 10 miles of the General Post Office in Lombard Street.

The reason for this is clear. The minimum rate for letters by the General Post was increased from twopence to threepence for a distance of 80 miles. By the Penny Post, ever since its beginning, a letter was carried for 1 d. within London proper, and another penny collected for delivery in the outskirts or the suburbs, to such places as Islington, Lambeth, or Hackney, which in those days were all separate towns. Therefore it was merely a matter of convenience whether a letter to such towns in the suburbs of London went by the Penny Post or the General Post—in either case the cost was twopence. Now that the minimum General Post rate was increased to threepence, it was necessary to define the range of the Penny Post, hence the 10-mile limit measured from the General Post Office.

Originally the Penny Post was limited to certain places "within the Weekly Bills of Mortality" (see p. 44). By 1690 the Penny Post circulated to any part of London or "any of the Towns or Villages round about it, for 15 miles"; and soon after it extended to places over 20 miles distant from London, to Beaconsfield in Bucks., and to Ongar in Essex.[1]

Limiting its range to 10 miles was the beginning of a gradual decline in the Penny Post service. Although continuing to be useful and still giving a service superior to any other public work, the high standard of its efficiency which was so notable a feature of its early years was not maintained. A letter written in 1765 to the *St. James's Chronicle* complains of the way letters were attended to by an old woman in Kensington. "Sometimes she is washing, sometimes asleep, and after 2 hours delay she deputes a Poorhouse boy, who can read no more than herself. Instead of arriving twice a day, letters come once; instead of at noon not until 10 at night, dirty and torn." Indeed, it would not be fair to accept this description as being typical, but the fact that it was allowed to happen is evidence that the administration was not what it was in the early days.

[1] See Appendix V, p. 170.

The Penny Post had become such an established occurrence in the everyday life of the Londoner that frequent and sometimes lengthy reference is made to it in the several guide-books and histories of the day; the almost affectionate praise bestowed upon it indicates the way in which people regarded it, a convenience enjoyed by all, by both rich and poor alike.

A visitor to England, Monsieur C. de Saussure, writing to his family in 1726 from East Sheen, near Richmond, Surrey, said:

> I think that I will do well to tell you of a few of the advantages of this city, for they are many, and are not to be found in other towns. Foremost amongst the number I must place the 1d. post, which is a most useful institution. It would be inconvenient in such a large town as London to have to run from one end of it to the other every time you had anything special to communicate. In order to provide for this difficulty, a large number of small offices have been established in every quarter of the town and in the principal streets. You may, if you wish it, write twice a day to anyone living in the town, and once a day to about one hundred and fifty small towns and villages in the vicinity of London. Should the letter be addressed to any place farther than London or its suburbs, the person who sends it, in giving it to be posted, will have to pay one penny, and the receiver will have to pay the same sum; but if the letter is addressed to the town or suburb the sender alone pays the penny. You can send parcels in the same way; a parcel weighing one pound costs no more than a simple letter. Whatever is sent by the 1d. post is well cared for, provided you have taken the trouble of registering it at the office, because should the parcel get lost, the clerk is in that case answerable for it.

Daniel Defoe, in his *Tour Through the Whole Island of Great Britain*, which was published in 1727, refers to the "modern contrivence of a private Person, one Mr. William Dockwraw (*sic*), now made a branch of the General Revenue of the Post Office". Letters, he says, could be sent—

> with the utmost Safety and Dispatch . . . almost as soon as they can be sent by messenger, and that Four, Five, Six to Eight times a day. . . . Nor are you tied to a single Piece of Paper, as in the General Post Office, but any Packet under a Pound weight goes at the same Price. . . . We see nothing of this at Paris, at Amsterdam, at Hamburgh or any other City, that ever I have seen or heard of.

In a little history called the *Survey of London and Westminster*, by Robert Seymour, published in 1735, we are told there were "above 600 Houses that receive for the Penny-Post, there being one in most great Streets; at the Door or Window of which is commonly hung up a printed Paper in a Frame, with these Words in large Letters, PENNY POST LETTERS AND PARCELS ARE TAKEN IN HERE".

At this point of the story it would be useful to mention an important development in the General Post organization.

After the Revolution of 1688 things seemed to open up more. The Post Office came under the Treasury, and it was no longer the aim to get as many letters as possible into or through London. There was more freedom in communication and news. Cross Posts began to develop, whereby letters could go by a more direct route between one town and another. It was difficult to account for the number of letters and the postage collected on those that did not reach London. The system was in fact wide open to fraud, both on the part of the country postmasters as well as the carriers, stage-coach drivers, and others. The heavy fines that could be imposed by the Act of 1711 did little to prevent this. And so we come to the first of two famous postal reformers of Bath, a very important city in those days.

Ralph Allen was a Cornishman who, as a boy, had helped his grandmother, who kept the post office in St. Colomb Major. In 1712 he became Postmaster of Bath, where he would meet and have to deal with the correspondence of many very important visitors. He thus gained an exceptionally good insight into what was happening throughout the postal system. In 1719 he proposed to the Postmaster General that he should take over and develop the Bye-way and Cross Road Posts at a rental of £6,000 a year,[1] and the following year his offer was accepted. That he proved himself a man of great ability there is no doubt, and the development of the posts throughout the country soon went ahead under his businesslike methods. By the time of his death in 1764, Allen had done a very great deal for the city of Bath as well as for his country. He had also become immensely wealthy and built the magnificent mansion of Prior Park (which is still to be seen today), where he entertained

---

[1] It was estimated that at this time these were bringing in a revenue of £4,000 a year. *History of the British Post Office*, Hemmeon (Cambridge) p. 36.

his many distinguished guests, among whom were Pitt, Gains-borough, Warburton, Fielding, and Pope. The latter's couplet on Allen is often quoted:

> Let humble Allen, with an awkward shame
> Do good by stealth and blush to find it fame.

And in literature, Fielding has immortalized him as the Squire Allworthy in *Tom Jones*.

This episode in our postal history is mentioned to show how far our Post Office was able to expand and benefit by the efforts and initiative of one man.

Following Ralph Allen's great achievement, the next important event was the passing of an Act in 1765 which permitted penny posts to be established anywhere within the realms of the General Post Office administration. But in granting this great concession an alteration was made in the Penny Post Office, reducing the weight of penny post letters or parcels to 4 ounces from the 1-lb. limit which had been in force since the very beginning.

By allowing penny posts to be set up in the provinces, the authorities doubtless hoped to repeat all over the country the same success which the Penny Post enjoyed in London, now established for over eighty years.

However, it was not until many years later that provincial cities and towns organized their own penny posts, Dublin being the first to establish one in 1773, followed by Edinburgh.[1] The beginning of Edinburgh's Penny Post was quite extraordinary and is another instance of individual enterprise.

It was begun by a man named Peter Williamson (see Plate 5), who, until coming to Edinburgh in about 1760, had lived a life full of adventure and remarkable experiences. The incidents in the early life of this man, who was to play such an important part in Edinburgh's postal history, are worth recounting, for to mention only his later life and his postal activities without a brief reference to his earlier days would give such a different impression of him.

When he was a boy of thirteen living in Aberdeen young Peter was unlucky to be kidnapped—a practice not uncommon in Scotland in those days. Along with some fifty other unfortunate children, he was put on a boat bound for America to be sold into slavery.

[1] See Appendix VII, pp. 178 and 181.

When the ship was in sight of Cape May, off the New Jersey coast, she grounded and was holed. The captain and crew, quite indifferent to the howls and shrieks of the children, took off in the ship's boat, leaving them to their fate, and safely reached the shore. Luckily for the children, the storm was not long in abating, for the captain, wanting to salvage what might be left of the cargo, sent some of his crew back. To their great surprise they found the children alive. Williamson relates in his diary how they were all eventually sold; he himself was fortunate to be bought by a Scottish farmer, Hugh Wilson, who as a lad had also been kidnapped and shipped to America. Wilson treated him kindly and took good care of him until he died, when he left Peter his best horse and saddle, £150, and some personal belongings. Williamson was now seventeen years old, and for the next seven years busied himself by taking what work came his way until he decided to marry. He chose the daughter of a well-to-do planter, who set him up in a 200-acre holding on the Delaware river, and all might have gone well for him, had it not been for the outrages then being perpetrated by the Red Indians.

At that time the redskins were being stirred into trouble by French settlers, who, coveting the British farmsteads, paid them as much as £15 a head for every British scalp, so as to get the British away and their land for themselves.

Williamson's homestead was attacked by Indians, his wife savagely murdered, and he himself was captured and taken away to live with the Indians. In his diary he tells of the most terrible tortures and cruelties he saw carried out on white farmers. He was forced to work for the redskins, and at times was tortured by having burning wood held near his face and body.

Eventually he escaped and lost no time in enlisting as a soldier against the French and their red allies. He now experienced another series of adventures. When Fort George was captured in 1756 he was taken prisoner and sent to Quebec, but after some time, food being scarce, and there being a shortage of guards, the French let their prisoners go. As one of a party shipped to England under a cartel, he arrived in Plymouth, and, being disabled by a wound in his hand, he was given his discharge and the sum of six shillings. With this amount in his pocket and with plenty of spirit he began to make his way back to his native Scotland. By the time he reached

59

York he was in pretty bad shape, but the account of his exploits aroused the sympathy of a gentleman there, who paid for his adventures to be printed in cheap form. By the sale of these, and the little money he made by exhibiting himself in Indian attire with feathered head-dress and uttering war-whoops, he earned sufficient money along the way to supply his needs until he at last reached Aberdeen.

Here he tried to get redress from those responsible for his kid-napping. He met with considerable difficulty, and his forthright remarks about the part played by certain merchants of Aberdeen (now prominent citizens) got him turned out as a vagrant, and he came to Edinburgh. He then took legal action against them, and although the process was tricky, he was successful and was given compensation.

In Edinburgh he set up a tavern in the vicinity of the Parliament, which became a rendezvous for lawyers and their clerks, litigants and idlers, and later opened an inn called "Peter's Tavern" in Old Parliament Close. It is probable that the busy coming and going which he witnessed of many of those engaged in the legal profession gave him the idea of a messenger service which a few years later he was able to organize.

He had become quite a character, and being of an ingenious turn of mind had invented a portable printing press on which he printed many of his works and broadsheets; another of his inventions was of stamps and ink for marking linen. His most famous work was the first *Edinburgh Directory*, which he published in 1773, continuing the series of them until 1796.

But his most important achievement was the organization of a Penny Post system for the whole of Edinburgh and district. Earliest mention of this is contained in an advertisement which appeared in the second edition of his 1774 *Directory*.[1]

Evidence shows that his post was begun some time between May 1773 and May 1774. His messengers, called caddies, wore a uniform, and letters were postmarked with the date they were posted. At first a straight-lined stamp was used. These are very scarce, only two copies being known. The usual type (and there are variations) show a circular stamp about the size of a penny, giving the date of

[1] See Appendix VII, p. 181.

posting and reading E. PENNY POST NOT PAID. A similar stamp, but very rare, is known for paid letters. These stamps have the appearance of being hand-made, and it is quite probable they were made by Williamson with the type used in his printing press.

Some time during the latter years of the 1780s he met with some competition when his second wife and his father-in-law attempted to set up an opposition post. Very little came of this, but as a consequence he divorced his wife in 1789.

Unlike William Dockwra in 1682, Williamson was never proceeded against; His Majesty's Postmasters General turned a blind eye towards his enterprise, so that his Penny Post remained in use for some twenty years. In actual fact it enjoyed semi-official recognition, for several letters that have survived showing his postal markings were sent by government offices, as well as by gentlemen attending the Court.

While on a visit to Edinburgh during 1790, Francis Freeling, the very able secretary of the Post Office, observed the usefulness of Williamson's enterprise; he saw also that it was a lucrative business, and the decision was made to have a government penny post in that city. This came about in 1793 when Williamson's post was taken over in its entirety and incorporated into the General Post Office of Edinburgh.

Williamson was treated very considerately, and no action was taken against him. Nor had he to petition the King or Parliament for a reward in recognition of what he had done.

In a letter dated July 19, 1793, the Postmasters General addressed themselves to the Treasury.

> We have also to beg your Lordships permission to authorise us to allow Mr. Williamson of Edinburgh £25 per annum, he having long had the profits of 1d. a letter on certain letters forwarded through his receiving house at Edinburgh, which he will lose by our having established a penny post there. We have made it a rule always to propose that those who suffer in their incomes from regulations which are certainly beneficial to the public should receive compensation for the loss they sustain.

This pension was granted to Williamson, and apart from the trouble with his wife, he led an easy and comfortable life in his old age. He had many friends who enjoyed his company, and was of a good-tempered though somewhat eccentric disposition. He died on January 19, 1799.

The Act of 1765 which allowed the setting up of penny posts all over the country also lowered the basic rate for a letter. By the Act of 1711 the charge for carrying a single letter up to 80 miles was threepence. It was now reduced to one penny for one stage and to twopence for two stages, a stage consisting of about 15 miles, more or less, the rate for longer distances remaining unchanged. Another change which the Act brought about was to limit the weight of letters and packages carried by the London Penny Post (and any other Penny Post that might be set up) to 4 ounces. As compensation for losses had long been abandoned, it is plain to see how little by little the benefits of the original Penny Post were diminishing as the years went on.

The Post Office itself was not altogether popular with the public, which resented the many irritating restrictions and new laws so often detrimental to the public's well-being. It sometimes happened when the public petitioned for an improvement in the service, for a new post to be established between towns or for some other purpose, authorities seldom tackled the problem in a businesslike way, but hedged and dithered, always putting obstacles in the way. Public opinion was aroused when it was disclosed during 1742 how sometimes letters were in the habit of being detained in the "secret room" of the General Post Office, where they were carefully opened and inspected before being sent on. Typical of the irritations was the ruling given in the Act of 1711 that every single letter or piece of paper which contained an enclosure (this could be a sample of cloth or a sample of seed) must be rated for double postage. Because of this, envelopes were never used, for a sheet of paper inside an envelope automatically incurred double postage.

It is easy to understand therefore how well remembered was Dockwra's name, for his service had never been improved on. Likewise, Ralph Allen, who had tackled and solved problems which had long baffled the General Post Office, and had improved the services with a well-organized and efficient cross-post system. The public must surely have realized that improvements in the postal services usually originated from the ideas and efforts of individuals like themselves.

A further great improvement which was to revolutionize the entire post office system happened in 1784, when John Palmer, the licensee of a Bath theatre, saw his plan for a speedier postal service begin with the setting out of the first mail-coach from Bristol to London.

Briefly, his plan was to have the stage-coaches carry the mails keeping to a scheduled time-table, thereby ensuring a speedier service than the post-boys could give. The Post Office should make contracts with the proprietors of all stage-coaches and to provide guards recruited from Post Office employees, suitably armed with blunderbusses, so as to prevent the highway mail robberies which had become all too frequent, the post-boys being easy targets for the "gentlemen of the road". The public would enjoy a speedier and safer mail service, and the Post Office would benefit by securing some thousands of pounds' worth of mail, which otherwise would be sent in parcels by the stage-coach to be delivered locally—a practice that had become quite usual with many large business houses in order to evade the high postage rates.

Palmer was able in 1782 to get an introduction to Pitt, then at the Treasury, through the good offices of an influential friend. This was most fortunate, otherwise such a great development of our postal services might have been long delayed. Pitt was very impressed with Palmer's proposals and instructed him to go ahead with the development of the plan, in spite of strong objections raised by the Post Office. But under a new ministry Pitt overruled all these, and in 1784 ordered Palmer to put his scheme into operation on the road between Bristol and London. On Monday, August 2, 1784, the first mail-coach, carrying four passengers (no "outsiders" were then allowed), a bag of mail, and an armed guard, left Bristol at 4 p.m. and arrived in London at 8 a.m. the next morning, exactly on schedule; and an hour shorter than the time taken by the fastest stage-coach. The service was daily and two way, the first down mail leaving London at 8 p.m. and reaching Bristol at noon the following day, five innkeepers supplying horses at suitable stages.[1] This accelerated the delivery of letters by a whole day. In the meantime,

[1] The name mail-coach was not used until later. The term used was mail diligence or machine. Likewise the term post-coach and post-chaise had nothing to do with the carriage of mail, and were names in common use before 1784

Anthony Todd, Secretary to the Post Office, had organized his plan of campaign to ruin Palmer and his mail-coach scheme. A very bitter struggle followed, which set back any immediate advancement to the scheme, and it was not until March the following year, and with further help from Pitt, that Palmer was able to extend the mail-coach service to other routes. For the next forty years or so the mail-coach became one of the outstanding features in the life of the country, creating what has been rightly called the Mail-coach Era. Palmer was rewarded for his unqualified success by being appointed, in 1786, Surveyor and Controller General of the Mails, at a salary of £1,500 a year. This appointment was by Treasury Warrant to the Postmasters General; so unfortunately Palmer's position was made even more difficult, and tended to play into the hands of his opponents. The end came in 1792, when Palmer's rather tactless behaviour, particularly with respect to the Postmasters General, led to his suspension. The mail-coach system could now very easily have collapsed, had it not been for the tremendous ability of Thomas Hasker, Palmer's Superintendent of Mail-coaches. Palmer was granted an annual pension of £3,000, which did not satisfy him, and like that other postal pioneer, William Dockwra, he spent his days petitioning Parliament for a bigger reward. He had certainly been responsible for many improvements while employed in the Post Office, and had proved himself an important man. Eventually in 1813 Parliament passed a Bill allowing him a handsome award of £50,000 in addition to his pension! He died in 1818.

By the end of the century the postal rates had approximately doubled, the Post Office being in dire need of revenue, and at the same time being bled for the several large pensions and other moneys it was called upon to produce. It was also during this period that penny posts—allowed by the Act of 1765—began to be more generally used. It has already been explained that a single letter for the first stage, a distance of about 15 miles, rated one penny. Now that coaches carried the mails, this penny rate was more commonly used, for it meant that a one-stage letter could be delivered quickly within a few hours, whereas formerly, when carried by foot-post or post-boy, it would be on a journey lasting the best part of a day.

With this penny rate no special stamps were used, the "One

Plate 4*a*. Peter Williamson, known as Indian Peter, because of his captivity and adventures among the redskins.

Plate 4*b*. Peter Williamson, the founder of Edinburgh's first Penny Post.

GENERAL POSTMAN.

Pub. by R. Ackermann, London.

Plate 5. A postman with a bell. About 1820. The penny he received for taking the letter to the General Post Office was his perquisite,

Penny" being written on by hand. But during the 1790s some of the larger cities, such as Manchester, Bristol, and Birmingham, which had opened penny post offices, stamped their penny-post letters with penny-post stamps, usually small circular marks with P.P. in the centre, and a number, which designated the office of posting. Manchester, on April 8, 1793,[1] issued a Post Office notice announcing the opening of four offices for letters and parcels not exceeding 4 ounces in weight, "One penny will be charged in the Town and two Pence for such as are for the Places adjacent and within the Penny Post delivery." There were five offices, the chief one situated in Back Square. The announcement stated also that deliveries would be made "all over the town" at 8 a.m., 12.30 and 6 p.m. Letter carriers were to take penny-post letters six days a week to Middleton, Ashton-under-Lyne, Staley-Bridge, Oldham, and Saddleworth "and other places of which due notice will be given".

Manchester's Penny Post proved a complete success, and brought in a gain of £586 for the first year. Both Bristol and Birmingham opened penny post offices soon after Manchester, and were likewise successful, both cities showing a fair profit for the year. It is really extraordinary that the Post Office, aware of the success of these provincial penny posts, moved so slowly and cautiously before opening up similar offices in other large provincial cities and towns; for the next one to be set up was in Glasgow, in 1800. Possibly the inaction was partly the fault of the local authorities.

Herbert Joyce, in his *History of the Post Office*, refers to the apathy of the Post Office at this time as incomprehensible, and describes the internal administration as deplorable. As a consequence of the American War of Independence, many of the colonial postmasters were back in England seeking pensions from an already overburdened establishment. Due to the war with the French the Post Office suffered grievous losses through the capture or sinking of many Packet boats; and to cap everything, there were disturbing rumours in circulation about corruption in high quarters. Indeed, as Joyce so aptly explains the situation, "the Post Office in more senses than one was falling about their ears".

By now, the year 1793, the London Penny Post, although capable

[1] See Appendix VII, p. 184.

of greatly increased business, had shown no increase in revenue for the past twenty years, notwithstanding a larger population and a considerable expansion of business within the city. This useful branch of the General Post Office had been shamefully neglected. Of its three "heads", it is said that only one, designated the collector, reported for duty, and even so, only occasionally. The other two, a comptroller and an accountant, never turned up at all! It followed that slackness was rife throughout its whole establishment.

Palmer, having introduced his mail-coach reform, and improved certain other functions of the service, was acutely aware of the slovenly way the Penny Post Office was being run, and applied to take it in farm, but his proposition was turned down. It was left to a former letter carrier, Edward Johnson by name, to take on the reform of the Penny Post Office. For some time Johnson had worked under Palmer, and, showing signs of more than usual ability, as well as being closely connected with Palmer, it was not long before he was taken notice of, and given a position of standing.

In 1793 there were, in addition to the very many receiving houses which served the Penny Post, five principal offices[1]—the chief office situated in Throgmorton Street, opposite Bartholomew Lane; the Westminster Office, in Gerrard Street, Soho; the Hermitage Office, in Queen Street, Little Tower Hill; the Southwark Office, in St. Saviour's Churchyard, Borough, and the fifth, the Temple Office, in Clare Market. There was very poor communication between these offices, and the letter carriers were never on time, so that punctuality in collection and delivery could never be relied upon. Types of the triangular paid stamps introduced by Dockwra were still used. A notice issued during the 1770s stated: "The triangular stamp on all letters and parcels shows the day they were brought to the Principal Office, and the round stamp the hour they are given to the letter-carriers".

Johnson proposed to have only two offices, the chief office, in Abchurch Lane, Lombard Street, and the Westminster Office, in Gerrard Street, Soho. He planned to increase the number of collections and deliveries and to serve all the districts of the Penny Post

---

[1] The exact location of these offices changed from time to time, but their general situation did not alter. The St. Paul's office seems to have closed down about 1769.

equally, the suburban places as well as the town, and to keep to a regular time-table, the hours of collection to be prominently displayed in all the receiving houses. Other improvements were devised as well, all aimed at providing the public with a speedier and more efficient service.

Fig. 10. *Types of London Penny Post stamps 1711–89.*
Many varieties are known.

The proposal to increase not only the number of letter carriers but also the staff of the Penny Post Office was regarded with alarm by the administration, for the additional expense which this would involve would seem to be far more than the office could carry. But the scheme was so skilfully introduced and contained such sound common sense that it was eventually settled upon, and in 1794 an Act was passed "For regulating the Postage and Conveyance of Letters by the Carriage called the *Penny Post.*"[1]

The rule which Dockwra had always insisted upon, that letters must be prepaid, was now waived in favour of optional prepayment. It is said the reason for this was because many messengers and servants entrusted with the money to take letters to the receiving house would pocket the money and destroy the letters! To meet this alteration in the law, new types of stamps were introduced; these were in use for only a few months.

The new law also allowed the Postmaster General to extend the delivery of letters by the Penny Post to a distance beyond 10 miles

[1] 34 Geo. III, cap. 17.

67

from the General Post Office at his discretion. The most important change of all was the charge of an extra penny on letters sent from a place in the suburbs to an address in either the City or Westminster, and vice-versa. The one-penny rate for letters posted in London,

Fig. 11. *Rare stamps used experimentally in 1794.*

Westminster, Southwark, and their suburbs to any place within these areas and their suburbs was still maintained. It was now that the receiving houses of the Penny Post (which were quite separate from those of the General Post) were given their own named stamps

Fig. 12. *Typical Penny Post stamps introduced in 1794–95.*

to be marked upon letters. Date-stamps, too, showing the time in full, were introduced.

Dockwra, in his day, had declared that one penny and no more would be paid, though it became common practice to give the letter carrier a penny on delivery to a place "outside the weekly bills of mortality" and a few years later when the Penny Post was under government control this extra penny was announced in many of the notices as being for the messengers "own Pains and Care". In the Act of 1711 it was stated only that letters by the Penny Post should be charged a penny, with nothing said about a penny on delivery; a subsequent Act of 1730[1] made the delivery penny legal. A charge of twopence was now imposed at the receiving houses or on delivery

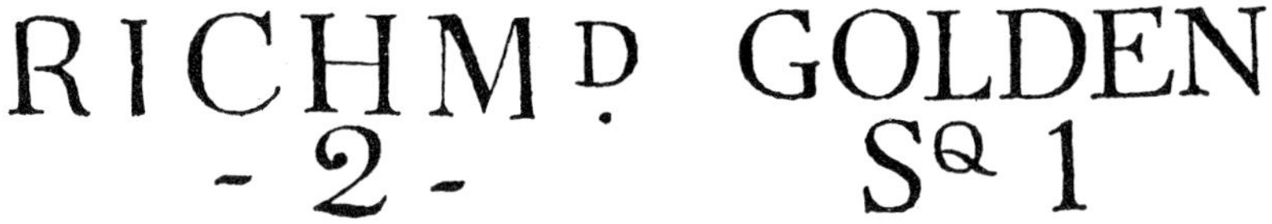

RICHM^D GOLDEN
- 2 -   S^Q 1

Fig. 13. *A new type of Receiving House stamp appeared in 1794 and remained in use for only a short time.*

for all letters sent to the country districts beyond the central area. Letters from the country districts and suburbs into the central area were now charged twopence, the second penny being paid on delivery. But letters for the General Post were still carried to and from the General Post Office for one penny, from any part of the Penny Post area, even to places in the suburban country districts. This may be said to be the beginning of the end of London's Penny Post, for in 1801 an Act of Parliament confirmed a twopenny rate on all letters, whether in the town or country area or passing to and from the General Post. Although the system went on as before, it was now known as the Twopenny Post.

A great boon was given to soldiers and sailors in 1795 when an Act[2] was passed allowing non-commissioned officers and soldiers, and petty officers and seamen of the Royal Navy (but not commissioned officers), whether stationed at home or abroad, to send and to receive their letters at the special rate of one penny. The concession applied only to single-sheet letters, and the penny postage was to be pre-paid; in the case of soldiers' and sailors' letters, the sender's name and rank had to be written along the top of the addressed side of the letter, which had also to show the signature of

---

[1] 4 Geo. II, cap. 33.
[2] 35 Geo. III, cap. 53.

his Commanding Officer. This special reduced penny rate remained in force until removed in 1920.[1]

So ended the eighteenth century, with the postal services greatly extended and speeded up, and with the General Post Office showing a real desire to help the public. Many of its officers were displaying a loyalty and zeal which hitherto had been rarely shown. Francis

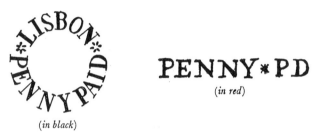

PENNY*PD

(in red)

(in black)

Fig. 14. *These penny hand stamps were used on letters sent by soldiers during the Peninsular campaign of 1812. (In the author's collection.)*

Freeling, the secretary of the Post Office, was a notable example and became one of its outstanding administrators. The muddle and apathy which had been so unpleasant a feature of its organization had been cleared away, largely under the guidance of Lord Walsingham, who had become one of the Postmasters General in 1789, a man who stood for no nonsense, whose integrity and high standards were markedly different from those of Lord Carteret, who had been one of the two Postmasters General for eighteen years until 1789. It is to him that much of the blame for the poor management can be accredited, also to Anthony Todd, who held the office of Secretary to the Post Office from 1768 for thirty-three years.

A factor which constantly remained to disturb everybody was the ever-increasing high rates of postage, and all manner of means were taken to evade them and to cheat the Post Office whenever possible. The one blessing was the way penny posts were being established in different parts of the country, a portent of even greater events that were to follow in the not too distant future.

---

[1] At the outbreak of both the Boer War and the First World War soldiers' letters on active service were charged one penny, but this rate was soon dropped in favour of free postage. Sailors, however, had to pay one penny on their letters during the First World War.

CHAPTER 4

Uniform Penny Postage

FRANCIS FREELING—HIGH POSTAGE RATES—ROBERT WALLACE,
M.P., AND POST OFFICE REFORM—ROWLAND HILL AND UNIFORM
PENNY POSTAGE—HENRY COLE—PENNY POSTAGE STAMPS

THE DIFFICULT AND vexatious years of the prolonged wars against the French brought about further increases in the postal rates; Francis Freeling, the Secretary of the Post Office, although a most able administrator, always took the view that the way to collect higher revenue was to make the public pay higher postage. London's Penny Post became the London Two-penny Post in 1801, with its limits cut down to a 3-mile area.[1] In 1805 all rates went up by a penny, and the same thing happened seven years later.

The one benefit which was enjoyed by everyone outside London was the steady growth of local penny posts throughout the length and breadth of the kingdom. Each year saw more towns and villages opening up a penny post office; the movement was at first gradual, then, between the years 1812 and 1815, the rush began, with penny posts opening up everywhere. Large cities such as Glasgow, Bristol, and Exeter operated penny posts to villages within their areas up to distances of 20 miles or so. The city of Bristol included about sixty sub-offices in its penny post area, Exeter served just under forty, and Glasgow more than thirty. By the mid-1830s penny post offices were operating throughout the entire United Kingdom. Whereas it was a costly business to send a letter some 30 miles distant or more by the General Post, the local posts were able to provide a splendid service for one penny—and this was a uniform rate for both letters and packages weighing up to 4 ounces. Even villages and hamlets remotely situated and away from the post roads were helped by a

[1] This was extended to a 12-mile area in 1833.

service called a "Fifth Clause Post", so named after the fifth clause of the Act of 1801, which allowed any village not belonging to a post town to petition to be linked up with its nearest post town—provided it was able to pay for the service. Thus, in the case of the Bristol district a Fifth Clause Post was established at Thornbury in 1825, and one penny charged for the delivery of each letter at Thornbury, which was made by a horse-post to and from Bristol.

However, apart from the excellent facilities offered by these penny posts, to send a letter farther away was at times quite a luxury for the ordinary person. The postage rates which had been settled by the Act of 1711 had remained in use until 1765, when a few reductions were made on short-distance letters. In 1784 they were all raised when Palmer's plan for mail-coaches was adopted, the Chancellor of the Exchequer explaining that the increases were instead of a tax on coal. The new mail-coach services increased the Post Office business enormously, and although the revenue rose in proportion, the postal rates were again raised in 1797, 1801, 1805, and 1812. In 1812 the charges for a single letter were:

Not exceeding 15 miles .	4*d.*
15–20 miles . . .	5*d.*
20–30 miles . . .	6*d.*
30–50 miles . . .	7*d.*
50–80 miles . . .	8*d.*
80–120 miles . . .	9*d.*
120–170 miles . . .	10*d.*
170–230 miles . . .	11*d.*
230–300 miles . . .	1*s.*
300–400 miles . . .	1*s.* 1*d.*
Over 400 miles . . .	1*d.* for every additional 100 miles

So that to send a letter from London to Brighton cost 8*d.*, and to Edinburgh, 1*s.* 1*d.*; considering the greater value of money of those times, it was often a matter of some concern to decide whether a letter was worth the amount of money it would cost. Indeed, the postage on a letter would sometimes represent a day's pay to a working-class man. This state of affairs remained until the end of 1839.

The whole machinery of the Post Office organization had become unwieldy and complicated. There were so many regulations, all of which were very involved, and quite apart from a scale of charges based on a fairly close table of distances, there were all manner of extra charges. For instance, an additional ½d. had to be paid on a letter going over the border into Scotland. A letter crossing the Menai Straits Bridge cost an extra 1d. A letter to Ireland could go via Holyhead cheaper than it could by way of Liverpool. Many London business houses sent their letters to Edinburgh by coastwise ship, which rated 8d. a letter instead of the 1s. 1½d. by road. A letter 1 ounce in weight was rated the same as four single-sheet letters; a letter written on a very small piece of paper and enclosed within an envelope was automatically rated at double postage, whereas a large sheet, folded over and across, would be charged as a single-sheet letter. It was small wonder that the public took every chance it could to evade the high postal rates. During the war years they had been regarded as an inevitable tax levied to help the war effort, but with the defeat of Napoleon in 1815 there was no relaxation, so that the high rates imposed in 1812 still prevailed. Bearing in mind that in those days it was usual for the recipient to pay the postage, it was an easy matter for a message to be sent without having to pay any postage at all. A young man, for example, away from home just starting work in London and wanting his family to know he was well, could simply address a blank sheet of paper to his parents, who, recognizing his handwriting, knew all was well with him and would refuse to accept it. People used pre-arranged codes whereby a mis-spelling in the address or an extra name or word added denoted a simple message.

Abuse of the franking system became more rife than ever. The privilege of franking letters free of postage had been confirmed to Members of Parliament and the aristocracy in 1656,[1] and, ever since, had been a heavy burden for the Post Office to carry, for the privilege had all along been much abused. Noble lords and members of the Commons would make presents to their friends of a few "franks"—letter sheets bearing their signatures; there were some

[1] A House of Commons order of September 29, 1656, directed "that the Post Letters directed to the severall members of this House be brought to the doors of this House and they be free from postage as formerly" (*Journal of the House of Commons*).

73

who became directors of banks and business houses in order to frank their firm's business letters, thereby causing a loss to the Post Office revenue of thousands of pounds annually.[1]

With advances made in education around this time, more children were growing up able to read and write, so the need existed for the public in general to have an easier and cheaper postal system. Newspapers and periodicals were now appearing more plentifully than before, and depended solely on the Post Office, which carried them free of charge, for their distribution.[2] They, too, were heavily taxed; what had been a tax of only a $\frac{1}{2}d$. in the time of Queen Anne was now $4d$., and each paper was required to show that the tax had been paid by having a red stamp printed on it. When in 1836 the tax was lowered to a penny the numbers of newspapers increased and greatly burdened the Post Office. One well-known publisher suggested at the time that the Government would find it easier to collect the penny tax by means of a stamped wrapper for the newspapers to be mailed in, but the Government took no notice of his idea. A few years later, when it was being decided how best to collect pre-paid postage from the public, his suggestion was remembered and considered a good one.

Inevitably with such a state of affairs, public criticism became loud—loud enough to penetrate the sacred mysteries of the internal workings of the Post Office. Many official inquiries into its management were held, and the Post Office was in bad odour. Since the time of Walsingham, other Postmasters General had not attended to their duties so conscientiously and had tended to leave everything

[1] The privilege of franking did not extend to the Penny Post organization.

[2] Since very early times, the distribution of news, and newspapers, was a Post Office undertaking. It was a long-standing privilege of the "clerks of the roads"—those in charge at the sorting office in the G.P.O.—to frank newspapers and to charge a fee to subscribers. This was a valuable perquisite of their office. In 1764 an Act of Parliament allowed newspapers franked with the name of a Member of Parliament to be carried free. This privilege was greatly abused, and during the early part of the nineteenth century things became worse when the Post Office permitted newspapers to pass free of charge with a Member of Parliament's name only printed on the wrapper. In 1834 all the Post Office officials were forbidden to sell newspapers, and in 1836 newspapers (with certain exceptions) went free when bearing the $1d$. tax. This early association with the Post Office explains why many of our national newspapers still have names such as "Mail", "Post", "Courier", etc.

to Francis Freeling, who had done so much good for the Post Office, but, being indifferent to public opinion, besides being rather an autocrat, he had always been an advocate of high postage rates. It can be said of him that he was one of the last of the old régime, to whom the inner workings of the Post Office were sacrosanct. With the deepest dismay he had to tolerate outsiders probing into its management. What they found was not very good, and although many improvements were made because of these inquiries, nothing was done to reduce the high postage rates. Sir Francis Freeling failed to understand what the public had to complain about. The mail-coach service was now in its prime, a highly efficient and splendidly organized service, with the mails speedily conveyed with regularity, and was superior to any postal service in Europe. Inquiry followed after inquiry, and the Post Office had lots of dead growth removed from its management as well as a good deal of trimming.[1]

In June 1836 Sir Francis Freeling died, a disillusioned old man. In some recent notes he had been working on was written:

> Cheap postage. . . . What is this men are talking about? Can it be that all my life I have been in error? To make the Post Office revenue as productive as possible was long ago impressed on me by successive ministers as a duty which I was under a solemn obligation to discharge. . . . Where else in the world does the merchant or manufacturer have the materials of his trade carried for him gratuitously or at so low a rate as to leave no margin of profit?[2]

The years of the 1830s were years of reform in other respects too. By the Reform Bill of 1832 a good deal of re-organization had taken place in the representation of the House of Commons; one result of this was for the town of Greenock to elect a young man named Robert Wallace as its first Member of Parliament. In 1833 Wallace made an attack on the Post Office with a speech which championed the need for Reform. To attack a State institution such as the Post Office, and to describe in blunt plain speaking a number of abuses in the administration that required to be removed called for great courage and exceptional qualities in a young man newly elected to

[1] During 1837 five new statutes took the place of over 100 out-of-date Post Office laws.

[2] He died a very wealthy man, for apart from his salary, his perquisites had been very lucrative. He was one of the most outstanding and important Post Office officials.

75

the House. His further speeches stirred and disquietened the House of Commons with his persistent criticisms, which provided facts and figures that convinced many of the need for reform. These constant criticisms, backed by proof of Post Office mismanagement and wasteful expenditure, brought about action, and inquiries were started into the Post Office management, which continued to the year 1837. As this year dawned an event took place which was to reshape the whole postal system throughout the British Isles and shatter the old régime; this was the publication of a small pamphlet by a former schoolmaster named Rowland Hill that quickly became one of the most controversial subjects of the day.

Rowland Hill was born in 1795, in Kidderminster, where his father owned a private school. Besides Rowland, there were five brothers and two sisters—all of them clever. From Kidderminster his family moved to Tottenham, where a larger school was opened by the Hill family in an old mansion called Bruce Castle, and in 1835 he accepted the position of secretary to the South Australian Commission, an organization concerned with promoting emigration to those colonies. He had always been interested in anything that concerned reform and public welfare. The speeches of Robert Wallace influenced him so strongly that he asked Mr. Wallace to lend him some books and papers that he might study the whole question of Post Office reform. Helped by advice from his brothers, Matthew, a lawyer, Edwin, an inventor, and Frederic, a writer on educational subjects, Rowland Hill set to work on the mass of books, statutes, and reports that Wallace had sent to him. The combined brains of these brothers, each of them singularly clever in his own way, probed into these papers and books sifting out the essential facts; figures and estimates were carefully calculated and conclusions were made which resulted in the publishing of Rowland Hill's famous pamphlet, *Post Office Reform, Its Importance and Practicability.*

Rowland Hill presented his case skilfully, reasonably, and with dignity. He started by showing how the revenue of the Post Office had been steadily falling in recent years in spite of high rates of postage and an increased population. He showed how the cost of managing the Post Office was too high for the amount of revenue it brought in. The many ways by which the public evaded paying postage were explained, and he described at length the abuses of the franking system. Although statistics and figures were not available, he was able to estimate the cost of carrying a letter from London to Edinburgh to be one-thirty-sixth of a penny, proving that the prevailing rate of 1*s.* 1*d.* was exorbitant. From an analysis made of all overheads and charges, he deduced that this cost of one-thirty-sixth of a penny could apply to a letter destined to anywhere in the kingdom. He presented arguments proving that a letter of moderate weight could be carried at a uniform rate to anywhere in the United Kingdom, and still be an economical proposition to the Post Office. He examined the whole question of Post Office management and staff, giving suggestions for improvement and economy. He showed how much time was wasted by the

Fig. 15. *A postman of the 1830s collecting postage on letters.*

letter carriers having to collect postage on the letters they delivered, and suggested the prepayment of letters by a uniform charge so that all this tedious work would be avoided. To quote from his pamphlet:

> There would not only be no stopping to collect the postage, but probably it would soon be unnecessary even to await the opening of the door, as every house might be provided with a letter box into which the Letter Carrier would drop the letters, and, having knocked, he would pass on as fast as he could walk.

The uniform charge he proposed was a postage of one penny per half ounce "for all letters received in a post town and delivered in the same or any other post town in the British Isles".

These proposals were received with great enthusiasm by the

77

public: newspapers and periodicals carried leading articles on the subject of cheap postage and Post Office reform; other pamphlets appeared written by supporters of Hill's plan, and so overwhelming was the demand for cheap postage that the Government was jolted into action. At the time Rowland Hill's pamphlet was published a Post Office Commission of Inquiry composed of Lord Duncannon, Mr. H. Labouchere, and the Duke of Somerset was sitting to examine the present condition of the Twopenny Post or London District Post, as it was known. As well as Wallace, Rowland Hill was invited to give evidence, and undoubtedly his opinions made a strong impression upon them. During the course of his examination he proposed that there should be a Penny Post, and when questioned about the Twopenny Post he suggested that this should be combined with the General Post and urged the adoption of several collections and deliveries daily within the London area. When asked his opinion on a suitable method of prepayment, he recalled the suggestion made by Mr. Charles Knight a few years previously that stamped wrappers be used for the purpose.[1]

> Let stamped covers or sheets of paper be supplied to the public from the Stamp Office or Post Office, as may be most convenient and sold at such a price as to include the postage. . . . Covers, at various prices, would be required for packets of various weights; and each should have the weight it is entitled to carry legibly printed with the stamp.[2]

The Commission recommended the adoption of a uniform rate of one penny per ounce and of twopence up to 6 ounces for the Metropolitan area of 12 miles around the General Post Office, making it a condition that special pre-paid stamped envelopes and covers should be used. Among those questioned was a paper manufacturer named John Dickinson, who described how he manufactured a special paper with silk threads running through the sheet as a prevention against forgery. This paper was used for Exchequer Bonds and other government documents and had been invented by Dickinson in 1828. It was manufactured behind locked doors at his Nash Mills, about half a mile from Apsley, near Hemel Hempstead,

[1] A pre-paid stamped letter sheet was in use in Philadelphia as early as 1836. Refer to p. 98.
[2] The Ninth Report of the Commissioners Appointed to Inquire into the Management of the Post Office Department, 1837.

on two machines always watched by Excise men. The silk threads were laid at equal distances in the paper, and when they broke, were mended by two women chosen for their trustworthiness.

When Rowland Hill proposed special pre-paid stamped covers Dickinson at once suggested the adoption of his paper for their manufacture. Envelopes at this time were not in general use, though a stationer named Brewer in Brighton is believed to have been the first to make them in England some time during the 1820s, probably because of the continental visitors in this fashionable seaside resort, who were accustomed to using them in their own countries, where they were not subject to extra postage, as was the case in England.[1]

In the Commission's published report were included specimens of an envelope and two covers made of Dickinson's special paper, and designed somewhat like a banknote with elaborate "engine turned" ornamentation. The penny envelope and cover were inscribed "London District Post—One Penny/Not to Exceed one Ounce" and were printed in pale sepia (see Plate 6). The Twopenny cover was inscribed "Twopence, To carry not exceeding 6 ounces", and was printed in green.

This Report was made in July 1837, and in November the endeavours of Robert Wallace resulted in a Select Committee being formed to study the question, carefully worded:

> To inquire into the present rates and modes of charging postage, with a view to such a reduction thereof as may be made without injury to the revenue; and for this purpose to examine especially into the mode recommended for charging and collecting postage, in a pamphlet published by Mr. Rowland Hill.

Those within the Post Office administration were appalled at Hill's proposals. The Postmaster General, Lord Lichfield, said "with respect to the plan set forth by Mr. Hill, of all the wild and visionary schemes which I have ever heard or read of, it is the most extravagant". Col. Maberly, the Secretary of the Post Office, who had succeeded Sir Francis Freeling, thought the idea preposterous

[1] Fanny Dickinson, writing to her brother in 1835, enclosed her letter in a "*pocket*", and on April 6, 1836, says she was busy "making envelopes all day" for invitations she sent out to a party. In her diary for July 1837 she notes "Envelopes at 2/6d per 100, to be had at 209 Regent Street". Envelopes at this time were not gummed, and were sold opened out; wax, or small wafer seals, had to be used to fasten the four corners together when the envelope was folded into shape.

and estimated that it would take some forty or fifty years for the revenue to make good the loss if ever penny postage were introduced. The Duke of Wellington was strongly opposed to the plan, believing that it would be the means of greatly reducing the Post Office revenue; but the bankers, the lawyers, industrialists, and business people were all in praise of it. Hill's pamphlet was so widely read that a second and a third edition were printed, each time the preface expressing a stronger criticism of the apathetic state of the Post Office organization.

With the Penny Post scheme now becoming so vast and far-reaching, it was understandable that Rowland Hill should ask for help, for his work in connection with the South Australian Colonization Commission was a full-time occupation. In February 1838 he approached Henry Cole, who had just completed much valuable work as Assistant Keeper of the Public Records, to help him. This was a most fortunate choice, for Henry Cole was an able, public-spirited man. A staunch advocate of penny postage, Cole was secretary of the newly formed Mercantile Committee of Postage, whose members were important and influential merchants of the City of London under the chairmanship of Mr. Joshua Bates, a partner in the banking firm of Baring Brothers. The Committee gave tremendous backing to the penny postage movement, organizing many public meetings and collecting signatures for petitions.

An ingenious and useful means of propaganda was devised by Henry Cole in the establishment of a newspaper called *The Post Circular*, the idea being that, registered as a newspaper, it would be carried free by the Post Office. Edited by Henry Cole, it made its first appearance on March 14, 1838, and was published solely to further the cause of Rowland Hill's reform and to champion the penny post movement. Altogether thirteen numbers were published and sent to a carefully selected section of the public, consisting of solicitors, doctors, town councillors, librarians, newspaper proprietors, and business people in different parts of the country. At first the Post Office refused to acknowledge it as a newspaper and charged it with postage, but following a letter written by Mr. Wallace to the Postmaster General, the Secretary, Col. Maberly, replied that the question having been submitted to the Solicitor and to the Postmaster General, it was decided that *The Post Circular*

Plate 6. A one penny pre-paid envelope for the London District Post
proposed in 1837. This was engraved in sepia on cream paper specially
manufactured by John Dickinson. Silk threads were laid diagonally in
the paper as a prevention against forgery.

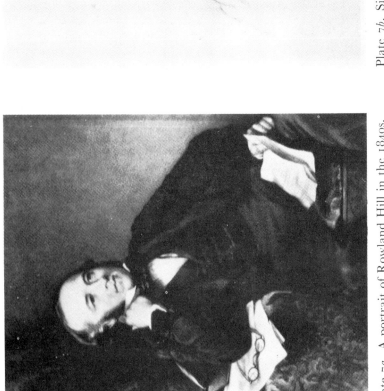

Plate 7a. A portrait of Rowland Hill in the 1840s. (*Courtesy of H.M. Postmaster General.*)

Plate 7b. Sir Henry Cole, K.C.B., from a drawing by S. Laurence. (*Courtesy The National Portrait Gallery.*)

was, in fact, a newspaper. This was a great triumph for Henry Cole, who exclaimed that the Post Office would now become the chief instrument of reforming itself!

Another device to show the absurdities of the rates of postage is described by Henry Cole in his autobiography.[1] He says:

> Two letters were prepared as already noticed by Rowland Hill, one being a large sheet of paper weighing under an ounce. If kept dry, it was charged only as a *single* postage, but if it became damp and turned the scale of one ounce even by a grain, it would be raised to four-fold postage. Another letter, weighing under eight grains, was also prepared. It consisted of two pieces of thin paper, and therefore was charged as a *double* letter. Fifty of each specimen were sent to the Charing Cross Post Office, by a clerk who had some humour. He produced first one of the largest letters. The clerk looked at it suspiciously. He held it before the lamp to see if it were really a single sheet. He summoned another clerk to help his judgement. All this caused a delay, and a crowd began to collect at the window, who watched the process with interest. At last the clerk marked it with a *single* rate, and the spectators laughed. Then the smallest letter was produced, and the Post Office official turned crimson, became furious, and cursed a little, but he could not help marking it *double* postage. Roars of laughter came from the crowd. Then fifty more of each letter were produced and marked, the large heavy ones with *single* postage, the little light ones with *double*. During the process the crowd impatiently filled up the whole of the pavement, and scoffed. No less amusement was produced in the House of Commons when Mr. Wallace exhibited the big and little letters.

This sort of propaganda had a telling effect, and together with cartoons, posters, and placards displayed in shop windows, Henry Cole's campaign was highly successful. The Mercantile Committee, too, busy in collecting a mass of useful information in support of the plan, was powerful in promoting the cause for uniform penny postage, so that very convincing conclusions were able to be submitted to Robert Wallace's Select Committee.

The Times referred to the movement as the "cause of the whole

[1] *Fifty Years of Public Life*, by Henry Cole. This public-spirited man was responsible for getting the nation's public records in order. He was one of the chief people connected with the Great Exhibition of 1851 and was active all his life in promoting art and culture to the public. Several museums were founded due to his efforts. He became a K.C.B. in his later years.

people against a small coterie of place holders in St. Martins-le-Grand".

It was not until February 1838 that the Select Committee was able to commence its sittings; presided over by Wallace, with Henry Warburton, the M.P. for Bridport, as secretary, it consisted of fifteen well-chosen members. For sixty-three days it listened to evidence not only from the Postmaster General and all the other senior officials of the Post Office but also to eighty-three independent witnesses of various walks in life, produced by Mr. W. H. Ashurst, the solicitor and parliamentary agent of the Mercantile Committee. Evidence was given also by Mr. Rowland Hill, later referred to humorously by Charles Dickens in *Household Words*,[1] "before the Committee, the 'Circumlocution Office' and Mr. Rowland Hill were perpetually in conflict on questions of fact, and it invariably turned out that Mr. Rowland Hill was right in his facts, and that the 'Circumlocution Office' was always wrong".

The findings of the Committee were presented to the House of Commons in March 1839. They agreed to a uniform rate of postage —though it was due only to the casting vote of the chairman—and proposed a uniform rate of twopence the half ounce. As for Rowland Hill's arguments, they concurred with his evidence that the high rates of postage interfered with trade and encouraged evasion of payment, and they recommended that the franking system be abolished. Among other conclusions made, they were of the opinion that a low uniform rate, combined with pre-payment by use of stamps or wrappers, would be useful and highly satisfactory to the public. Although they could not foresee any immediate loss through the adoption of a uniform penny rate, they were not in a position to recommend any plan that might cause such an eventuality; therefore they restricted themselves to the recommendation of a uniform twopenny rate.

The public's clamour for a uniform penny post persisted. Its imagination had taken to the idea of a penny post. It was used to the penny posts now in operation all over the length and breadth of the kingdom. There was a popular *Penny Magazine* and a *Penny Cyclopaedia*. Penny-a-day schools were not uncommon, and there were many other "pennyworths" to be had; it was the beginning

[1] *Household Words*, August 1, 1857.

of an era of pennyworths, so that the idea of a uniform penny post seemed natural even to the more unthinking members of the public.

The Mercantile Committee continued its activities, organizing public meetings in various large towns and collecting signatures to petitions. One particular petition bearing 12,500 names, all collected in one day, was presented by the Lord Mayor and citizens of London. By July 1839 some 2,007 petitions bearing 262,809 signatures were presented to Parliament.

In June 1839 Rowland Hill issued another pamphlet *On the Collection of Postage by means of Stamps*, followed by another the next month entitled *Facts and Estimates as to the Increase of Letters*, in which he predicted an increase of letters passing through the post of five times during the first year of the plan. In a monthly issue of Charles Dickens's *Nicholas Nickleby*, a small pamphlet was enclosed describing an imaginary scene at Windsor Castle with the Queen questioning her Postmaster General and Lord Melbourne. It concluded with the Queen suggesting the dismissal of Lord Lichfield, the Postmaster General, and recommending the adoption of Hill's plan. This particular pamphlet, the work of Henry Cole, was most popular, and was reprinted in many forms.

The general wish of the public showed itself so manifestly that, finally, a hesitant and reluctant government introduced a Penny Postage Bill in August 1839. Pre-payment was to be made by means of stamped envelopes or stamped paper just as soon as a uniform penny postage could be arranged. It can be said that Rowland Hill's pamphlet had brought about more upheaval and reform within the Post Office than all the Inquiries and Reports put together.

There were, of course, some who could see no good in the scheme, especially senior staff in the Post Office administration and certain members of the Government who were to lose the privilege of franking. Among those who made a serious objection—not against the scheme itself, but against the suggestion that stamped letter sheets and covers were to be provided by the Government for sale to public—were the stationers and paper makers. They protested against what they were assured would be a government monopoly, and also at the much cheaper price the stamped paper would be

Penny Postage.

The town of Bridgwater was favoured last week with an **ADVERTISEMENT** setting forth the evils dreaded by the *Conservatives* from the adoption of a measure highly beneficial to the Nation. — And herein they act consistently. — For those greedy gentlemen, who wish to *Conserve* all the good things of Providence to their own Pockets, cannot possibly wish to promote the general happiness and welfare of the Nation at large.

One *wise* reason which has been given by the Conservatives is That it would deprive their Representatives of the privilege of bestowing the favour of Franked Letters. ●━● So, likewise, a Plan for promoting general health, would deprive our Doctors of the privilege of bestowing on us the favour of their physic. The fact is, We pay dearly for both. *See Somerset County Gazette, July 27th,* 1839.

But there is nothing like **A TORY'S OWN WORDS.** He says,

" The Measure will, if carried, chiefly benefit those persons who pay little or no direct Taxes, such as Labourers, Domestic Servants, and Persons in the humbler classes of life. To those in high stations, and of large fortunes, the relief will be of no importance. "

Here then we have it, **OUT AT LAST.** ●━● The Tory Principle, All Abroad, in their own Hand-Bills! *That the Conservatives oppose a Cheap Postage, because it will only benefit the Poor who want it!* And it is the Poor who indirectly and ultimately pay all Taxes. The Tory Principle is now out, as clear as Mud. *That Taxes are to be laid on the Poor, and not on the Rich.*

The Tory Advertiser further asks, *How is the deficiency of Revenue to be raised?*

We shall find no deficiency. Yet whenever you want money, Our Answer is ready enough. Lay your taxes on the *Rich,* and not on the *Poor.* On *Riches acquired,* and not on the *means of acquiring riches:* —— of which Rail-Roads, Free trade, and a Cheap Postage, are amongst the most important.

The Advertiser proceeds to say, *That a* Cheap Postage *will not benefit Shopkeepers, and other Tradesmen, because they all either do or ought to take good care to charge the expense of* Postage *on their* Customers.! Rob Peter to pay Paul. This is Letting out the truth in good earnest. Let the Public look well to this. 'Tis amazing, or rather, 'tis not amazing, to witness the deep ignorance of those who can see on one side only.

As to the Revenue, it will not be diminished by the new system of Postage; it will be much increased thereby, both directly and indirectly: — the number of Letters sent will be so much increased: as every man of business knows. Thus it will enable the People to pay more to the Conservatives, both Whig and Tory. Money in both pockets. So that they may join all together in the same song.

Here's a Health to old honest John Bull.

Clark, Printer, Bridgwater *July 27th,* 1839.

Fig. 16. *A propaganda poster of 1839.*

sold, envisaging a loss of business from which they could never recover. Their arguments were published in a two-page pamphlet entitled *Penny Postage—Case of the Paper Makers and Stationers, Calmly Considered.* One of the blessings cheap postage was to bring was the facility it would offer the poor man of obtaining a cheaper piece of writing paper at the Post Office than he had ever before been able to buy.

One publisher, Mr. J. W. Parker, suggested how the stamped covers could be put to useful purpose by tradesmen having lists of their wares published on the inside, and thereby circulated cheaply through the post.

The immediate problem that now confronted the Government was how best to provide a convenient means of pre-payment by the public, which, at the same time, would be practical and economical to organize. It was decided to invite members of the public to give their suggestions by participating in a public competition. On August 23, 1839, the Treasury announced the terms of the competition to artists, men of science, and the public in general, and asked for proposals for the best means of using stamped covers and postage stamps to serve on letters, having regard to convenience, adequacy, and security against forgery. An award of £200 was promised for the best proposal and £100 for the next best, with a time limit imposed of three months. It is recorded that about 2,600 designs and suggestions were offered, of which only forty-nine referred to postage stamps.

After the Penny Postage Bill was passed, Rowland Hill resigned from his post with the South Australian Commission, on being appointed to the Treasury to supervise the introduction of penny postage. His appointment was a temporary one of two years, and, as he remarked in his diary, he was offered a position at first greatly inferior in prospects to that which he was giving up, but he accepted it in order to see his project properly launched. Following a very well and carefully composed letter addressed to the Chancellor of the Exchequer, his salary was increased from the suggested £500 to £1,600 a year! The decision to place him in the Treasury, instead of in the Post Office, was made because it was known how very unpopular he was with the General Post Office officials. For an assistant he applied for and obtained the services of his staunch

85

supporter Mr. Henry Cole, who understood so well the intricacies of the new undertaking (see Plate 7*b*).

After presenting himself to Mr. Francis Baring, the Chancellor of the Exchequer, one of the first duties Rowland Hill carried out was to visit the General Post Office in Paris, so as to make himself acquainted with the method used for the weighing of letters, and to see the kind of weighing machines employed; for the French Post Office, unlike the British, rated their letters by weight and not by distance. In his journal he records how impressed he was with the general efficiency of the French Postal officials, with their methods of stamping, sorting, and delivery. As was the case with all things he did, Hill made a very thorough inspection, and returned to London on October 16, after a fourteen-day visit.

The weeks that followed were crammed with all manner of problems to be worked out, and Hill had besides to interview and consult the many people concerned with the manufacture and design of the new stamps and covers.

The examination of the suggestions submitted for the Treasury competition (see Plate 8) occupied well over two months of valuable time. None of the suggestions or designs was considered suitable. In fact, many were quite absurd, though several were very ingenious. Four were selected for their merit, and the prize, which had been increased to £400, was divided among them in equal shares of £100. These four competitors were all Londoners: James Bogardus and Francis Coffin, who sent in a joint attempt and were awarded £50 each; Benjamin Chevington, of 72 Pratt Street, Camden Town; Henry Cole, of Nottinghill Square; and Charles Whiting, of Beaufort House, Strand.

The design finally decided upon was from a sketch Hill himself had suggested, and his idea of stamped letter sheets and envelopes was also approved. More than once during the campaign for the Penny Post he proposed the use of adhesive stamps, although at the time the idea of the use of stamped envelopes and letter sheets was the chief consideration. When giving evidence before the Duncannon Commission in 1837 he suggested the use of "a bit of paper just large enough to bear the stamp, and covered at the back with a glutinous wash which the user might, by applying a little moisture, attach to the back of the letter". In the second edition of his

86

pamphlet[1] Hill gave to Charles Knight, the publisher, the credit for the idea of the use of stamped wrappers.

Stamps of a sort had long been employed for fiscal purposes, but the earliest suggestion for an adhesive postage stamp seems to have been made by James Chalmers, a bookseller of Dundee. In 1837, prior to the Treasury competition, he had manufactured circular adhesives as essays, and in the *Post Circular* of April 1838, in support of Hill's plan, Chalmers wrote a letter advocating the use of little gummed slips of paper in preference to stamped envelopes. He suggested they could be printed in sheets, to be cut as required and affixed to letters by wetting the backs of the slips.

The design for the postage stamp had been sketched for Rowland Hill by the artist Henry Corbould, the central design being the Queen's head taken from the very beautiful medal by William Wyon which was struck to commemorate the Queen's first visit to the Corporation of London at Guildhall on November 9, 1837 (see Plate 11*a*). It was decided to show the Queen's head in the design to overcome any attempt at forgery, for it was believed that a forgery of the engraved head would be spotted more readily. The work of engraving the head on the die was given to Charles and Frederick Heath, father and son. An engine-turned background such as was used for engraving bank-notes was made by the printers Messrs. Perkins, Bacon, and Petch, who used a special hand-made water-marked paper for the work. After two attempts made in providing a suitable die a number of proofs were made, until at last in April 1840 the proof of the first penny plate was produced, with the lower corners left blank. This, signed on the back by Rowland Hill, is in the possession of the General Post Office. Essays for the stamp and some of the proofs are contained among the papers in the Henry Cole Bequest, to be seen in the Victoria and Albert Museum; others are in the Royal collection, and a few are in private hands.

The stamps were printed in black from eleven plates. Some of these plates, particularly plate eleven, are scarce; others have small distinguishing marks which collectors look for. This to some extent explains why high prices are sometimes paid for certain specimens,

---

[1] The first edition, a shorter one, was privately printed and headed "Private and Confidential".

whereas, by and large, ordinary copies of the penny black stamp are common and worth very little.

As a further protection against forgery, a little watermark of a small crown showed on each stamp, and to prevent the re-use of old stamps by joining together unmarked pieces, check letters were inserted in the lower corners. The stamps were printed in twenty rows of twelve stamps, making 240 stamps on a sheet. The first stamp was lettered A A, the next one A B, and so on, to the twelfth stamp, which was lettered A L. The next row began with the letters B A and so on for each of the 240 stamps in the sheet. As these check letters were stamped on by hand, positional variations and slight marks sometimes occurred, which collectors look for. The stamps were divided by a narrow margin to allow each stamp to be separated by being cut with scissors, for it was not until many years later that stamps could be torn away by means of little perforations. Experiments were made with a machine for dividing the stamps in 1848, and in the early 1850s the first attempts at perforating were made, but it was not until 1854 that Henry Archer's invention for perforating stamps was adopted for general use.

For the stamped envelopes and letter sheets Mr. Henry Cole was asked to obtain a suitable design. Following his preliminary inquiries among members of the Royal Academy, Cole approached Mr. William Mulready, R.A., at the special request of the Chancellor of the Exchequer. Mr. Mulready promptly agreed to the proposal, and within a few days provided an allegorical design showing a somewhat bewildered Britannia bestowing the gifts of cheap postage to the four quarters of the earth, while the benefits of letter writing were enjoyed by those at home (see Plate 9a). Sufficient space was left for the name and address to be written in the middle of the design. For this "highly poetic design" (to quote Henry Cole) the special paper invented by Dickinson was used with silk threads running through it as security against forgery.

Interviewing and consulting the many people to be concerned with the manufacture of the stamps and letter sheets proved difficult and tiresome for Rowland Hill; all were specialists, and all proved awkward to work with, as they had their own ideas about how things should be done, and these new adhesive stamps and envelopes were not only novel but also required to be manufactured in a certain

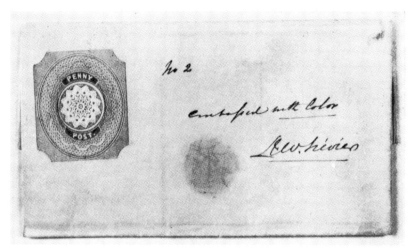

Plate 8*a*. An entry submitted by Robert W. Sievier for the Treasury Competition. Engraved in brown, red, and blue. (*Author's Collection.*)

Plate 8*b*. This design, which exists in brown, vermilion, yellow, and blue, was submitted by James Wyld, who was geographer to the Queen. The examples are to be found among the Henry Cole papers. (*Victoria and Albert Museum.*)

Plate 9*a*. The Mulready Envelope.

Plate 9*b*. Caricature of a Mulready Envelope.

SOLD HERE,

THE POST OFFICE

LETTER WEIGHT,

FOR ROWLAND HILL'S PLAN OF PENNY POSTAGE,

REGISTERED PURSUANT TO ACT OF PARLIAMENT, 2 Vic. c. 17.

PUBLISHED BY HENRY HOOPER,

AT THE

POSTAGE DEPOT,

13, PALL MALL EAST, LONDON.

Plate 10. The first Letter Weigher made for the Penny Postage. At the suggestion of Henry Cole, this design was registered in August 1839. Later, many contraptions of ingenious design came on the market. (*Victoria and Albert Museum.*)

Plate 11a & b. The Wyon medal (*left*). The Queen's head was taken from this for the "Penny Black" stamp. Throughout her long reign it was not changed, and the name of the country has never been shown, a tradition that remains to this day.

Plate 11c. The first Christmas card, devised by Henry Cole in 1843 and published by him under the name of Felix Summerly. Cheap postage made Christmas cards possible.

way. His task was made the more difficult by the animosity of many of the Post Office officials who were supposed to co-operate with him. At times his orders were wilfully misunderstood, stupid mistakes were made, and he received little help and the barest civility from Col. Maberly, the Secretary of the Post Office, who frequently showed his dislike of Hill by his rudeness and indifference. A series of set-backs was encountered too from the people connected with the printing and preparation of the new stamps, especially from the Stamp Office, where his younger brother Edwin was employed in superintending the manufacture of the letter stamps, so that valuable time was lost.

Entries in his diary show that Hill felt the strain very much, for he refers repeatedly to days when he was compelled to stay at home because he was feeling unwell.

The first step towards a penny postage was announced to an impatient public to begin on December 5, 1839, when an experimental rate of fourpence per half ounce was introduced throughout the British Isles, pre-payment still being optional. Rates lower than fourpence remained unchanged except in London, where under the London District Post the rate was reduced to one penny. The one penny charge made for letters carried over the Menai Straits Bridge, as well as the extra halfpenny levied on letters crossing into Scotland, were abolished. This proved to be a wise move on the part of the Post Office, for it permitted all its offices and workers to become accustomed to a uniform charge by weight instead of by distance. But the public were so insistent for uniform penny postage to begin that the Government was compelled to announce its commencement for January 10, 1840, before either the new stamps or stamped envelopes were ready.

The centuries old privilege of franking came to an end on January 9, 1840, but specially printed envelopes were made available for Members of the House of Lords and for Members of Parliament. One was printed in red with the imprint "(Temporary)" above the inscription "To be posted at the House of Lords only. Post Paid.— ONE PENNY.—Weight not to exceed $\frac{1}{2}$ oz". Another, printed in black, was similarly worded for posting at the House of Commons but without the word "(Temporary)", and a third was printed for the Houses of Parliament. Twopenny envelopes were also issued. These were in use for only a short time until the new adhesive penny stamps were available, and are eagerly sought after by collectors, because of their rarity.

The entry in Hill's diary for January 10 reads:

> Rose at 8h.20m. PENNY POSTAGE extended to the whole Kingdom this day! Very able articles on the subject in the *Chron. Advertizer*, and the *Globe*. The Tory papers for the most part sulky. *Standard* abusive of the C. of the Ex. and lying as to the cause of delay in the stamps. The C. of Ex. much pleased with Matthew's admirable article on Postage in the *Edinburgh Review* published yesterday. I have abstained from going to the P.O. tonight lest I should embarrass their proceedings. I hear of large numbers of circulars being sent, and the *Globe* of to-night says the P.O. has been quite besieged by people prepaying their letters. I guess that the number despatched tonight will not be less than 100,000, or more than 3 times what it was this day twelve months. If less, I shall be disappointed.

He was not disappointed, for 112,000 were posted. On this day also the privilege of franking ceased, the Queen herself expressing the wish that the rule should apply to her letters as well. Henceforth only official mail was to be carried free.

An idea of the enthusiasm shown by the public on the opening days of the new Penny Post is given in an article written by Henry Cole for the May number of the *Westminster Review*:

> A night or two after the change to a penny we ourselves witnessed the scene at St. Martin's le Grand. The great hall was nearly filled with spectators, marshalled in a line by the police to watch the crowds pressing, scuffling, and fighting to get first to the window. The superintending President of the Inland Office with praiseworthy zeal was in all quarters directing the energy of his officers where the pressure was greatest. Formerly one window sufficed to receive letters. On this evening six windows with two receivers at each were bombarded by applicants. As the last quarter of an hour approached, and the crowd still thickened, a seventh window was opened, and that none might be turned away Mr. Bokenham made some other opening, and took in money and letters himself. To the credit of the Post Office not a single person lost the time; and we learnt that on this evening upwards of 3,000 letters had been posted at St. Martin's le Grand between five and six. A witness present on the first night of the Penny Post described to us a similar scene. When the window closed, the mob, delighted a

the energy displayed by the officers, gave one cheer for the Post Office, and another for Rowland Hill.

The weeks following were vexing and difficult for Hill, for the new stamps were taking a long time to produce.[1] His relationship with some of the Post Office officials—as well as with the Stamp Office, who were working with him—continued to be strained; the only person who was at all times gracious and considerate towards him was his immediate superior, Mr. Francis Baring, the Chancellor of the Exchequer.

On May 1, 1840, the new stamps and envelopes were ready and put on sale to the public, who were instructed not to use them until May 6, the date proclaimed for their first day of use.

The new penny postage stamp, printed in black, proved popular and was well received by the public, but Mulready's design on the envelope and covers was ridiculed right from the start. Writing in his diary on May 12, Rowland Hill admitted that his idea of an artistic design was an unfortunate one. He wrote:

> I fear we shall be obliged to substitute some other stamp for that designed by Mulready, which is abused and ridiculed on all sides. In departing so widely from the established "lion and unicorn" nonsense, I fear that we have run counter to settled opinions and prejudices somewhat rashly. I now think it would have been wiser to have followed established custom in all the details of the measure where practicable. The conduct of the public, however, shows that although our attempt to diffuse a taste for fine art may have been imprudent, such diffusion is very much wanted. If the current should continue to run so strongly against us, it will be unwise to waste our strength in swimming against it, and I am already turning my attention to the substitution of another stamp combining with it, as the public have shown their disregard and even distaste for beauty, some further economy in the production.

Many years later, Henry Cole in his autobiography said:

> After forty years' additional experience, I agree in the soundness of the public opinion expressed, that this fine design was quite unsuitable for its purpose. . . . The postage cover was for a dry commercial use, in which sentiment has no part.

[1] See Appendix VIII, p. 189.

In *The Standard* for the evening of May 2 appeared one of the earliest criticisms:

THE NEW POST OFFICE STAMPS

We have now lying before us specimens of the envelope, and of the affair—for we do not know what else to call it—with the "glutinous wash".

The first is a half sheet, or somewhat less, of letter paper, on the front of which appears an outline sketch that is not very easy to describe. In the centre, perched on a lump of mud, in the midst of a mill-dam, or pond, is a figure of Britannia, sitting, as it would seem, though one can't see upon what; a shield reclines against her knee, and a lion, with a particularly unleonine physiognomy, at her feet. The lady's arms are extended in the act of letting loose certain winged animals, but whether angels, or quite the reverse, is by no means clear. . . . To the lady's left we see certain American Indians shaking hands with some odd-looking people in mackintoshes; a female with an infant in her arms, "doing maternal" under a cocoa-nut tree; a gaunt person, wearing a sombrero, and apparently giving orders to a cooper who is at work on a hogshead, and at least half naked; while another individual altogether so, sits upon the ground doing nothing. What concern any of these have with the penny postage passes our comprehension; but we take it for granted that Mr. Baring knows, or, beyond a doubt, Mr. Rowland Hill. . . . A word or two touching the stamp with the "glutinous wash", and we have done. It is a little square bit of paper, about three-quarters of an inch long by half an inch broad, and as it chanced to be reversed when we first saw it, in the innocency of our hearts we mistook it for a patch of German corn-plaster. However, on turning it over, we saw it contained what purports to be the head of Her Majesty, very ill-executed, with the word "Postage" above, and "One Penny" below. This badge is to be affixed on the right hand of the address of the letter, and in the upper corner. . . .

So much for the description of what has been universally acclaimed as the world's most beautiful postage stamp, for it is generally acknowledged that no stamp has ever been issued that surpasses the famous "Penny Black" in simplicity of beauty or design (see Plate 11*b*).

It is said that Queen Victoria was very pleased with the stamp, which is borne out by the fact that the same youthful profile was used throughout her long reign. The only words that appeared on the stamp were "Postage One Penny". Nothing more was required, for there was no other postage stamp in the world. Today this tradition remains with the British Post Office. The stamps of Great Britain do not show the country's name, only the sovereign's head, which is sufficient to carry them to any part of the world.

In *The Times* of the same date, May 2, the Editor remarked:

> We have been favoured with a sight of one of the new stamp covers, and we must say we never beheld any thing more ludicrous than the figures or allegorical device by which it is marked with its official character—why not add embellished? Cruikshank could scarcely produce anything so laughable. . . .

Innumerable rude and sarcastic letters were written in like vein to all the principal newspapers, some referring to Mr. Mulready as "Mulled-it-already", or "Mullheaded". The human tendency is to remember the rude and the comical in preference to the serious; in all fairness, it must be stated that many notices in praise of the designs appeared in several papers, principally those of Liberal outlook.

The new envelopes were quickly lampooned by caricaturists, and many of these comical designs have survived, greatly prized by collectors. These show more than anything else how the Mulready envelope was ridiculed out of existence (see Plate 9*b*).

The new Penny Post introduced other novelties too; the public now had to be aware of the basic half ounce weight, so ingenious letter-weighing devices were put on the market immediately uniform penny post started. These were of all shapes and sizes, and, as a rule, were made of brass and sometimes highly ornamental (see Plate 10).

The new envelopes were not gummed, they were required to be sealed by wax or wafer. Quickly the little French-made wafers were introduced for sale in the shops, *Pains de cacheter* they were called, but soon little coloured wafers were being manufactured in England and sold in attractive little boxes or envelopes with pretty designs and mottoes on them. Some of the earliest showed sentiments such as "A Penny for your Thoughts" and "Thank Rowland Hill for This". Many were used to further propaganda for Free Trade, the Repeal of the Corn Laws, for Temperance, and for any popular movement. Sometimes a slogan would incorporate the Penny Post, such as one which appeared for Temperance: "The nutriment in a gallon of ale, which has cost 2*s.* is not worth a penny!"

A new article in the way of stamp boxes appeared in the shops. The earliest were usually made of Tunbridge ware, little boxes with a design of coloured wood in mosaic, showing the Queen's head in the form of a postage stamp on the lid. Envelopes, too, were a novelty for the public, and quickly became very popular. Until now, the mere fact of enclosing a letter inside an envelope would have incurred extra postage, so that they were never used except occasionally by those having the privilege of franking. Now, envelope manufacturers printed them with charming ornamental designs, often in colour, around the borders, or embossed them with elegant lace-like decoration, suitable for special occasions, such as birthdays and St. Valentine's day.

Enterprising people were quick to take advantage of the advertising possibilities offered by the new Mulready covers, by having the inside sheet printed with small advertisements, and selling to the public at prices greatly below the one penny value of the covers, a practice which the authorities stopped after a few weeks. Many businesses saw the possibilities of cheap and efficient advertising by having their names and business printed inside their own covers, a practice which soon extended to envelopes, so that envelopes were often covered back and front with a pictorial representation of a firm's business. Some of these have survived today as charming examples of Victorian art, and are much sought after by collectors.

Cheap postage and the use of envelopes now permitted small articles to be sent by the post; in 1843 a few people used Christmas cards for the first time. Britain's first Christmas card was the idea of Henry Cole, and was published by him under the name of Felix Summerly. Hand-coloured, it was about the size of a small postcard; only 1,000 were published, so that examples today are very difficult to find (see Plate 11c). The artist who designed it was J. C. Horsley, and showed a homely family gathering sitting down to a Christmas dinner, the whole surrounded by a rustic trellis decoration, with "A Merry Christmas and a Happy New Year to You". Although quite an innocent card, and produced with the best of motives, it met with sharp criticism from some quarters, as having a dissipating influence, for the grown-ups in the picture were shown drinking wine!

Valentines—which had been in vogue for many years—now, thanks to the Penny Post, enjoyed an even greater popularity. But it was

94

not until the latter part of the 1850s, after a cheap process of colour printing was invented, that Christmas cards and all other kinds of greetings cards were used in really great numbers. At this time they were about the size of a visiting card, embellished with a simple though tasteful decoration. Penny Post was also responsible for increasing the popularity of pictorially headed note-paper. Note-paper showing beautifully engraved views of nearly every resort and place of interest in the kingdom, especially seaside places, as well as decorative motives and comical designs, was published in small sizes suitable for enclosing in envelopes. These were the forerunners of our present-day picture postcards.

These were but some of the additional items responsible for increasing the business of the Post Office. But although there was an expansion in business, there was a sharp fall in the Post Office revenue, and Rowland Hill was forced to admit that his original calculations were not proving accurate. It had been confidently expected that the greater business brought to the Post Office would soon off-set the expected deficiency of the first year. But things were not proving that way, and Rowland Hill was faced by a hostile postal administration waiting for time to prove how right they had been.

In 1841 there was a change of government, with the Tories, led by Sir Robert Peel, in office, and Hill half expected to be relieved of his position. But he was kept on, and retained as an adviser to the Treasury until dismissed in September 1842. He tried hard to remain in office, protesting that it was necessary for the success of his plan and for the reforms he required to carry out in cutting down expenditure that he should be given a position in the Post Office. His case was listened to very sympathetically by a Committee appointed to study it, but its conclusions went against him. He thereupon published, in 1844, his other well-known booklet *The State and Prospects of Penny Postage*, in which he refuted the statements of many of the Post Office officials given in evidence during the case, and attempted to prove by a fresh set of figures the success of his plan, over a longer period of time. With another change of government in 1846, Rowland Hill eventually got himself into the Post Office, under the Liberals, when he was made secretary to the Post-master General, Lord Clanricarde.

CHAPTER 5

Achievement in the United States

THE EFFECT OF PENNY POSTAGE OVERSEAS—AMERICAN RE-
ACTION–AMERICAN CAMPAIGN FOR POSTAL REFORM—THE NEW
YORK PENNY POST—AMERICAN LOCAL POSTS AND CARRIERS'
SERVICES—REDUCTION IN POSTAGE RATES PROCLAIMED IN THE
UNITED STATES

ACROSS THE CHANNEL, Britain's new experiment was regarded with great interest. A few countries sent representatives over to make reports on the working of the new Uniform
Penny Post, and although the general opinion was that Britain had
been rash to adopt a uniform rate so low as one penny, many
countries began to introduce reforms and lowered postage rates,
though none took the risk of reducing to a charge so low as a penny,
and only a few ventured to reduce the charge to a rate comparable
to about twopence. These reductions, however, in some cases permitted lower rates to come in force on correspondence to and from
Great Britain.

The first European country to copy the idea of adhesive stamps
was Switzerland, when the Cantons of Zurich and Geneva introduced
them in 1843. Overseas, Brazil followed suit in the same year. By
the early 1850s the majority of European countries, and many
States overseas, as well as the British colonies, were using postage
stamps. Worthy of note was New South Wales, which had used a
pre-paid envelope in 1838 for local postage in Sydney, thereby
getting ahead of the Mother country in that respect. Rowland Hill's
postal reforms, therefore, can be said to have reached nearly around
the globe; but other countries, having the benefit of Britain's initiative, were more cautious in keeping to a higher rate, for even by
1850 the Post Office revenue was still lower than it was in 1839.
On the other hand, it was dealing with a vastly increased business
and was giving the public a very wonderful service.

96

Plate 12*a*. A pre-paid cover used by J. W. Buchanan of Nuneaton. (See Appendix VIII, page 189.) (*Author's Collection.*)

Plate 12*b*. A unique caricature. Rowland Hill, backed by his supporters, is shown defying his opponents, while John Bull congratulates him. (*Author's Collection.*)

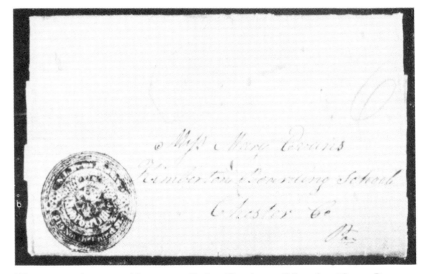

Plate 13*a*. A pre-paid cover of the Northern Liberties News Rooms, Philadelphia, 1836. (*Courtesy John A. Fox, New York.*)

Plate 13*b*. A letter carried by the New York Penny Post which began in January 1840. (*Author's Collection.*)

Right from the start the Post Office of the United States had been very interested in Rowland Hill's plan, and in June 1840 sent over their "special agent", Mr. George Plitt, to study and report on the London Post Office. Mr. Rowland Hill wrote in his journal, "he appears to be intelligent, and well selected for the mission".

Britain's new Penny Post had been a subject of envy among large sections of the American public, who had an expensive postal administration with postal charges nearly as high as in Britain, and a franking system very similar. Consequently, there was no lack of writing to the Press and drawing attention to the subject by articles on the need for Post Office Reform. Petitions were presented to Congress to abolish the franking system and to reduce the prevailing high rates of postage. But their demands came to nothing.

In the annual Report made by the Postmaster General, Mr. Kendall, to the President in 1840 he said:

> The radical change in the rates of postage on letters, recently adopted in Great Britain, has attracted much attention in the United States. To enable me to furnish Congress with information on the subject, and all others connected with the post establishments in several of the most considerable European countries, I have despatched one of the special agents of this department to Europe, with instructions to visit them in person, and furnish me with minute details of their organisation and operations. . . .

The reaction to this brought forth angry retorts in the United States Press on the need to send over to Europe a "special agent", when all the information required about the London Post Office could be obtained in the many books and reports already in circulation. It was asked what he had been doing for nine months, that "he has not yet been able to prepare himself to make a detailed report? This special agent left New York in the *Great Western*, last June, still he has not given sufficient information to enable the Postmaster General to report on this interesting subject!"

It was pointed out how the cheap postal system had been in operation in England several months, "and even despotic sluggish Austria, has followed the example", yet their energetic and industrious Mr. Kendall had done nothing except to send over a special agent, who, after a nine months' laborious research, had not yet been able to understand the system so as to make a full report.

97

The Press called the attention of the public to the position in England, where the Post Office was expected to provide revenue towards a heavy national debt and enormous government expenses, yet even so "with a promptitude that does the Lord Commissioners infinite credit, they have reduced the postage to a cheap and equal rate throughout the United Kingdom".

The United States Post Office was never intended to be a source of revenue to the country's Treasury; it was expected to support itself and to provide a useful and adequate service to the public. For in those early days there was a strong case for the Post Office to be operated at a loss in order to maintain effective communication between populous centres and far-flung communities in more remote places. Also it was considered necessary that a postal deficit should be supported out of taxation in order to advance the level of education and competence in a nation having universal franchise.

In recent years the Post Office was running at a heavy loss, and at this time was in debt to around half a million dollars. But the public's imagination, filled with the picture of England enjoying a uniform penny postage, persisted in its demands for a cheaper postal system and for the franking privilege to be abolished. The situation, however, was vastly different in the United States, where distances between towns were infinitely greater than in England, serving a much smaller population, so that the American people's argument in comparing the state of things in their country with conditions in England was not a reasonable one.

Similar in some ways to the provincial and country penny posts of Great Britain, were the "letter carriers" services which were allowed to function in the United States by a law of 1825. There were letter carriers in Philadelphia for several years prior to the Act, and probably in other cities as well; in Albany, N.Y., a carrier was working as early as 1808, though whether officially appointed or not is not known, but later he was and served for several years. Beginning in 1836, a private post in Philadelphia issued specially printed letter sheets, corresponding in a way to pre-paid covers (see Plate 13*a*). This "sub post office" was at the Northern Liberties News Room, a meeting-place for merchants and businessmen, situated in the district of Northern Liberties, some three-quarters of a mile north of the government Post Office, which was in the

98

Merchants Exchange Building. Patrons of the News Room would buy these letter sheets on which to write their letters, their cost including the charge for taking them to the Post Office.

The official city delivery services instituted by the Act of 1825 were undertaken by "carriers" under a bond given to the United States Post Office for the faithful performance of their duties. The local fee usually made on the letters they carried was two cents, about equal to a penny. Where there was no official letter carrier service privately organized services were set up, sometimes competing with the government posts. They commonly called themselves Penny Posts, and the earliest known was the one established in New York in 1840, called the "New York Penny Post". An early reference to it appears in a notice in the New York *Journal of Commerce* of December 20 and December 21, 1839:

> The New York Penny Post Association respectfully give notice that they commence business on Monday first, referring to their Prospectus, which is being extensively circulated, for the particulars of their plans. Being the first to attempt the establishment of a Penny Post in America, they hope to receive such a liberal support at starting, as will encourage them to persevere. 62 Canal Street.

The editorial of the same paper said of this venture:

> *Free Trade Penny Post.*—An association has been formed for the purpose of distributing letters and small packages through the city in the manner of the "Penny Post". They have announced some seventy-five places where letters and packages may be deposited, and which will be emptied and the packages carried to their destination twice each day. Each package will be stamped with the hour, and be taxed, three cents, to be paid on delivery. We can easily conceive that such an association may be one of great usefulness in a city where ten thousand messages are to be sent daily in all directions. The worthiness of the association to be trusted is attested by the names of a dozen of our most respectable individuals and firms.

This was purely a local post serving the immediate neighbourhood of the city of New York. The term "a penny" was commonly used in North America, and especially in the Eastern States, and denoted a very small amount, usually one or two cents, according to circumstances. The one-cent coin is still colloquially referred to as a penny. Not much is known about the New York Penny Post, or those who organized it. Letters carried by it were postmarked with a circular stamp reading "New York—Penny Post" with the date in the middle (see Plate 13*b*). It lasted into 1841, then another, under the name of "The New York City Despatch Post", started in February 1842, operated by Alexander Greig. Its functions were explained in a circular:

New York City Despatch Post
Principal Office, 46 William Street

The necessity of a medium of communication by letter from one part of the city to another being universally admitted, and the Penny Post, lately existing having been relinquished, the opportunity has been embraced to reorganize it under an entirely new proprietory and management, and upon a much more comprehensive basis, by which Despatch, Punctuality and Security—those essential elements of success —may at once be attained, and the inconveniences now experienced be entirely removed.

The circular further explained that letter-boxes would be conspicuously placed in every part of the city, and that all letters not exceeding 2 ounces in weight would be collected and delivered three times a day. The cost was three cents, whether prepaid or not, but for the convenience of prepaid letters, adhesive stamps were available at a cost of thirty-six cents a dozen, to be affixed to the letters to show they had been paid for. These postage stamps, privately made, were the first to appear in the United States,[1] and were actually the first to be issued in another country following the example of Great Britain's penny black stamp.

This City Despatch Post was at 46 William Street, in the financial district. In August 1842 it was taken over by the Government and its name changed to United States City Despatch Post. It operated for a while from the United States Post Office near the City Hall Park until the Post Office and the Despatch Department were moved to Nassau Street some time in August 1844. In 1846 it was discontinued and was succeeded by another which was also short lived. An important private post at this time in New York which operated a two-cents (one-penny) business was established by Aaron Swarts

[1] Postage stamps issued by the United States Post Office Department did not appear until 1847.

at Chatham Square in 1847 and became one of the largest local posts in the city until 1856, when this, too, changed hands.

It is not unreasonable to suppose that the initiative in organizing and starting a Penny Post in New York on the part of public-spirited businessmen was inspired by the demand for cheap postage following upon the postal reforms which had just taken place in England.

For by now the special Post Office agent had returned from Europe and had presented his report to the Postmaster General. He proposed that the United States should have two rates of postage, 5 cents ($2\frac{1}{2}d$.) for the first 500 miles, and 10 cents for longer distances. This was indeed an improvement, as at present the rates were graded, starting with 6 cents for 30 miles, and increasing by mileage up to $18\frac{3}{4}$ cents for 400 miles, and over 400 miles—25 cents. But the Government took a long while digesting these proposals and public agitation continued.

More and more private posts and carriers' services were set up in most of the important cities of the United States; the local posts, usually under the name of a penny post or a despatch company, were entirely operated through private enterprise, while the carriers were sponsored by the United States Post Office. There were besides, numerous private posts which operated over long distances—Independent Mail Routes that owed their origin chiefly to the high rates of postage under the 1825 Act of Congress and to the unsatisfactory management of the Post Office Department. The Government tried to suppress these enterprises, but loop-holes permitted them to operate, and the general public, as well as commercial houses and business firms, appreciating the better service and the cheaper rates, naturally patronized them in preference to the official posts. Whenever possible these independent posts operated along the most populous mail routes, thereby hitting the government service where it hurt the most.

Among the better-known operators of these private posts were the American Letter Mail, which operated between Boston, New York, and Philadelphia; Hale and Company of Boston; Pomeroy's Letter Express in New York State; and Harnden and Company, who carried letters from New York to Boston for the fast steamships to England.

The public supported the Independent Mails by holding mass

meetings and agitating against using the government mails until the government rates of postage were reduced. This came about in 1845, when two rates of postage were introduced—five cents for a half-ounce letter up to a distance of 300 miles, and ten cents for over 300 miles. These rates were more or less what the Independent Mail services had been charging, and as the "Private Express"

1853. Hartford (Conn.).

1855. Printed in black on a buff envelope.

1856. Newark (N.J.).

1855. The California Penny Post Co.

Blood's Penny Post was the largest delivery company in Philadelphia, begun in 1841 by D. O. Blood and Co.

1850s. A carrier's date stamp of the U.S. Penny Mail, Philadelphia.

Fig. 17. *A selection of United States Penny Post stamps.*

section of the Act of 1845 made the operation of private mail carriers over United States post routes illegal, the Act put the Independent Mail Routes out of business. Prior to July 1, 1845, when the Act became effective, the rates by distance were for one sheet of paper. An envelope with one sheet of paper was regarded as two sheets and was rated double postage. Consequently—as was the case in Britain before the advent of uniform penny postage—envelopes were not in general use and only became possible when the 5-cent and 10-cent rates per half ounce came into force.

The private posts which operated in the principal cities continued their useful work in providing local delivery services. During the 1850s they were making profits collecting and delivering mail in half the time and sometimes at half the prices charged by the Post Office carrier service. One of these local posts was the California Penny Post Company, which was set up in 1855 by J. B. Goodwin and partners. At first it operated to San Francisco, Sacramento, Stockton, and Marysville. Later, branches were opened in Benicia, Coloma, Nevada, Grass Valley, and Mokelumne Hill. It was essentially a city delivery post, bringing mail to the General Post Office and receiving mail for local delivery. The company issued envelopes, some bearing the government three-cents postage stamps impressed, others requiring the regular United States postage stamps to be affixed. Its system was to forward letters which had been enclosed within the company's special envelopes which carried an instruction along the top "TO THE PENNY POST CO". A small panel next to the postage stamp contained "PENNY-POSTAGE PAID, 7" (sometimes "5"). A variety showed a large panel with the instruction "To the Post Office, Care of the Penny Post Co." superimposed over a large "Paid 2". Severl types of these Penny Post envelopes are known with different inscriptions; all are very scarce. The California Penny Post Company did not remain in business for long, for it obviously infringed the rights of the Post Office, and was suppressed.

The Post Office Department tried to monopolize the city post business under an Act of 1851, but again was unable effectively to do so because of loopholes in the law. Eventually most of the private posts which had operated where there was also an official carrier were compelled to close down by an Act passed in 1861. Exceptions were the private posts of Boyd's and Hussey's in New York; these two posts were able to continue until 1883, but the reason why is not clearly understood. The postal laws did not affect places or routes where no government service existed, which is why some enterprises survived until the 1880s. There was a private post in Chicago until 1864, and another in Atlantic City, N.J., until 1887. A few sporadic local posts started up during the 1880s in several cities, notably in St. Louis, Chicago, and New York. Why they ever attempted to operate cannot be explained, for they were all quickly suppressed.

Of the several well-known penny posts were Blood and Co. of Philadelphia; Boyd's City Express of New York; the Broadway Post Office of New York; Swarts' City Despatch Post of New York;

Browne & Co. of Cincinnatti; the Chicago Penny Post; Floyd's
Penny Post of Chicago and the One Cent Despatch of Baltimore and
Washington. There were many more. They issued their own postage
stamps and had their own penny post date-stamps and cancellations.

In 1863 a uniform rate of 3 cents was introduced throughout the
United States regardless of distance, and in the cities a local letter
rate was fixed at 2 cents (i.e. a penny rate.) All carriers' fees were
abolished. This came about through the work of the Postmaster
General, Montgomery Blair who did more than any other American
Postmaster General to bring about reforms and improvements. He
played a big part in the preliminary work towards the formation of a
Universal Postal Union, and due to his initiative a conference was
convened in Paris on May 11, 1863, when the idea and its problems
were discussed. When it is remembered that he drafted these postal
laws, and worked on the idea of a Postal Union when the country
was in the midst of a civil war, and involved in extra heavy expenses
incurred by the war, it is the more to his credit that he was able to
achieve so much.

But the American people were to wait another twenty years before
they got a uniform penny postage at a 2 cents rate. As was the case
in England, the people learned that persistent agitation, along with
private enterprise, gave them what they wanted.

CHAPTER 6

The Campaign for Ocean Penny Postage

ELIHU BURRITT WAS born December 8, 1810, in New Britain, Connecticut. He was one of ten children in the family of a hard-working and poor smallholder, whose forebears had come from Glamorganshire before 1650. On his father's death, Elihu Burritt (see Plate 14) apprenticed himself to Samuel Booth, the village blacksmith, and, to make up for loss of adequate schooling, set about educating himself. He attended the local school, but as absence from work cost him about a dollar a day in wages, he began to teach himself at the anvil. He studied mathematics and amused himself by tackling problems of mental arithmetic while working at the forge. Gifted with a remarkable memory, his mental prowess developed so rapidly that he was able to solve quite difficult problems in this way.

His elder brother Elijah, a graduate of Williams College and a mathematician of some standing, encouraged him and helped him in his studies, so that by the time Elihu was twenty-one he was able to devote himself to more intensive study. He quickly mastered Latin and French, and then began to learn Greek. He would carry a small Greek grammar in his hat, to which he would refer while at work in his forge.

This quest for knowledge eventually took him to the University of Yale in Newhaven, where, with neither teachers nor tutors but only the atmosphere of the college and his own determination, he mastered not only Greek but also Spanish, Italian, German, and Hebrew.

Having become so proficient in languages, he tried teaching in a small academy, but after a year he left and tried one job after another before finally resuming his old occupation of blacksmith in the Massachusetts town of Worcester. Here his great joy was in being able to visit the library of the Antiquarian Society, which contained a valuable collection of rare books. He spent much of his spare time studying text-books on ancient languages and, coming across a Celto-Breton dictionary and grammar, he became so interested that he felt he had to master it. After much hard work and study he composed a letter in that ancient language and sent it to the Royal Antiquarian Society of France. In reply he received a most laudatory letter which testified to the correctness of his composition, the first and only letter in the Celto-Breton language to be written from America!

He was now acquainted more or less with all the European languages as well as some of Asia, including such difficult tongues as Chaldaic, Samaritan, and Amharic. Believing that he should turn these accomplishments to some useful purpose, he wrote to William Lincoln, a prominent citizen of Worcester who had befriended him, outlining the circumstances of his life and what he had done. Somewhat to his amazement and great discomfort, for Elihu Burritt was a very shy man, his letter was forwarded to the Hon. Edward Everett, the Governor of Massachusetts. Governor Everett thought so well of him that he received a certain amount of publicity. Several well-to-do citizens of Boston, including Henry Longfellow, the poet, offered to send him to Harvard University to complete his studies, but any suggestion of pecuniary help he declined, preferring to go his own way and to remain independent. It was now that people referred to him as "the Learned Blacksmith", a nickname that stayed with him for the rest of his life, and often he was invited to lecture, the public enjoying a sight of this intellectual wonder. His lecture was entitled "Application and Genius", his theme being that all attainments were the result of persistent will and application. This made such a profound impression on people that he was invited to give it no less than sixty times in one season to audiences in New York, Philadelphia, Baltimore, and several other places. Such was his nature that at the conclusion of this strenuous lecture tour he returned to the blacksmith's forge in Worcester, where, working again at the anvil, he prepared in his mind another lecture for the next season.

About this time he became occupied with philanthropic ideals, which led him to ponder over the possibility of a real bond of brotherhood between all peoples of the world. He started a weekly paper called *The Christian Citizen*, devoted to the ideals of peace, anti-slavery, and the brotherhood of man; although its circulation was not large, it attracted a certain amount of attention as being the first newspaper in America devoted to the cause of peace, and Burritt, encouraged by the interest shown in it, started a movement known as "The Olive Leaf Mission".

It was just at this time that the question of the Oregon boundary began to create bad feelings in the relationship between Great Britain and the United States; so much so that an actual rupture between the two countries at one time seemed imminent.

Public-spirited men in both countries rallied together in a campaign to stop the surge of bad feeling. They were inspired by the sincere endeavours of an earnest peace-loving Quaker, Joseph Crosfield of Manchester, who organized the sending of a series of "friendly addresses" written by hand from towns and cities throughout the United Kingdom. These were signed by the leading inhabitants, addressed to people in American towns, calling upon them to do their utmost to end the controversy by peaceful means and stressing an ardent desire for peace and friendship. Leading citizens, such as Cobden, Bright, Douglas Jerrold, and Charles Dickens, lent their support to the cause, the American newspapers giving their letters much publicity; "friendly addresses" from America were also given prominent notices in the British Press. These letters from Britain were sent to Elihu Burritt, who forwarded them to their many destinations. To help further their cause, through greater publicity, he sent copies of them to a great many of the principal newspapers of the United States. Two letters in particular, which he considered of special merit, he took to Washington, where it is said they made a deep impression in official circles.

Elihu Burritt's concern and activity in the cause for peace and preservation of friendship between the two countries had brought him into touch with similar-minded gentlemen in England. He therefore made up his mind to visit them, contemplating a visit of about three months. He sailed for England in May 1846 on the very steamer which was bringing the news of the satisfactory settlement of the Oregon Question.[1]

In England he was acclaimed by a large circle of friends and admirers, and it was not long after his arrival that, with the sympathy and support of friends in Birmingham and Manchester, he formed the nucleus of a movement called "The League of Universal Brotherhood", dedicated to promote friendship and good relations between countries and to work for the abolition of war. He was soon speaking in tightly packed halls, not only in London but in towns and cities throughout the kingdom. In some cases, it is said, the meetings were so crowded that he had difficulty in making himself heard.

His lecture ended with the reading of a pledge, the signing of which made every man or woman a member of the association. In less than a year several thousands of people both in England and the United States had signed this pledge, and in May 1847 the League of Universal Brotherhood was formally organized in London, and recognized as one of the many benevolent societies of the day. Thus was created in the mind of this remarkable American what was to be the first League of Nations.

One of the first interests of the League was to organize a campaign "for the abolition of all restrictions upon international correspondence and friendly intercourse". At the time rates of postage between countries were very high; few international agreements existed, and a letter posted overseas would sometimes cost several shillings. The basic rate of postage at this time on a letter between Great Britain and North America was one shilling or twenty-four cents.[2] To many people this amount was prohibitive, particularly to the thousands of poor people who were at this time emigrating from Great Britain, and especially those from Ireland. It meant that they could not keep in touch with their families and friends.

The story is told of a letter coming from one of the colonies to an

---

[1] Oregon was occupied by the British in 1814, but was claimed by the United States Government, to whom the greater part was ceded, after much negotiation, by a treaty dated June 12, 1846.

[2] This was the rate on letters carried by the official government packet—the Cunard steamships. When carried by other ships, the price was eight pence, but the time taken was longer.

old lady in England, who was unable to pay the postage on it, so it was sent back to the colony. In the meantime the poor woman to whom it was sent died in the workhouse; and enclosed in that letter was £25 for her support. Another poor soul received a letter from Australia, the postage unpaid on it amounting to 3s. 2d. She had to pawn her shoes and cloak in order to get it.

During February 1847 Burritt had witnessed for himself the distressing state of affairs in Ireland, where due to the recent potato crop failure, there was famine, poverty, and terrible disease prevalent everywhere, and it left a lasting impression on him. On his return to England he landed at Liverpool, where he saw a miserable and unhappy crowd of famished Irish labourers with some of their friends and families who had come to say good-bye to them, about to leave by steamer for America. Burritt describes the heartrending farewells of these poor people, driven from their country by starvation and sheer necessity.

> . . . Never had I witnessed, even at the bed of death, such agonising expressions of affection. Men gaunt and clad almost in rags embraced each other, and with arms interlaced around each other's necks, exchange adieus as if annihilation would soon lie between them. The whole multitude followed the steamer as far as the extremity of the dock, weeping and wailing with an exceedingly bitter cry.

This, and the harrowing scenes of misery he had witnessed in Ireland, stimulated him more than ever to agitate for a cheap overseas postage. For such poor wretches as these and many thousands like them, he well knew, could never afford the cost of a letter to keep them in touch with their loved ones.

His first move was to write to the most important man in the United States, known personally to him, the Hon. Edward Everett, Governor of Massachusetts, who replied by letter dated May 31, 1847:

My Dear Sir,

> It gives me sincere pleasure to receive a line from you by the last steamer, and to learn from it that you are labouring with so much life and heart and with such success in the cause for Peace. Your project of a foreign penny postage is admirable. All the reasons in favour of such a postage at home apply with equal force to international postage.

109

AN OLIVE LEAF FOR THE ENGLISH PEOPLE.

OCEAN PENNY POSTAGE.—No. 2.

Of all nations upon earth, England alone is able to establish an OCEAN PENNY POSTAGE.

If merely a brilliant abstraction, or splendid conception of genius, were necessary to effect an enterprise of vast consequence to mankind, then it would be of slight importance to ascertain the physical strength, the pecuniary means, the rank in society, or even the locality, of the man from whose mind the great idea was to originate. But when the necessities of the age require a stupendous work to be done, which must involve, in its execution, not only the concentrated energies and affluence of a well-developed mind, but also the most vigorous exercise of the powers of a well-developed body—a work which not only requires the combination of these two classes of executive faculties in one man, but in a man occupying a particular rank in society, a particular location of residence, and a particular range of influence and pecuniary means—then all these qualities of condition and ability become indispensable. The very rareness of their combination in one person, involves the person who possesses them in a responsibility from which he cannot escape.

The social tendencies and commercial necessities of mankind are converging into the want of an

Ocean Penny Postage.

To meet this world's want must be the work of *one* nation, in order to give an energetic integrity to the enterprise : and that nation must be distinguished from all others by its relative position, its physical constitution, the character and condition of its population, the genius of its language, its industrial and commercial economy, the constitution of its government, its material wealth and pecuniary resources, its present and prospective relations with the rest of the world. All these distinctive qualities are indispensable in the nation upon which this vast enterprise must devolve. If America or China possessed them all but one; without that one, neither of them could do this work for the world. If the steam and other mercantile navy of America were ten times its present tonnage, it could not send ocean postmen to England, to take England's letters to Alexandria, Bombay, Calcutta, or to any seaport of India or China. If China had a steam navy of more tonnage than all the navies of the rest of the world put together, she could not carry the letters of England and France to America. Both those nations, and all others similarly situated, must for ever lack the faculties of local position, which England alone possesses, to establish an

Ocean Penny Postage.

The nation that shall work out this desideratum of the age must be singularly qualified for the undertaking, by the conformity of the genius of its population to the physical constitution of its territory; both of which must distinguish it from

Fig. 18. An Olive Leaf dated March 1847.

There is, I suppose, a vague idea, that to give up the one shilling sterling on American letters would be favouring us, at the expense of the English revenue. It is very doubtful whether it would eventually prove a losing arrangement. But if it were, the saving to the individual payers of postage is, at any rate, as much for the benefit of England as of America. In favour of a foreign penny postage, there is one circumstance that does not apply to domestic mails. The great multitude of cheap letters has increased the expense of transportation. The service is more costly. But Mr. Cunard's shoulders are broad and strong; and you may increase the number of mail-bags twenty fold without tiring him.

I hope you will meet with entire success in this excellent move of yours. I have spoken of it only as a matter of expense and accommodation to the business world; but I can scarce think of anything which would give so much new life to all international communication,—and contribute so much to the formation of a *Public Opinion of the Civilised World.*

I remain, with the most friendly wishes,

Yours faithfully, Edward Everett.

By September 1847 he had developed his idea of an Ocean Penny Postage, his plan being that one penny only should be for the service of carrying a letter by ship, in any direction and for any distance, with an inland postage of one penny and two American cents added, making a total of threepence.

Burritt's intended visit of only three months had now become indefinitely prolonged. He had become a public figure, his whole time given up to ideas and schemes devoted to the welfare of others, especially to those in less fortunate circumstances.

He was a great believer in the distribution of ideas by means of tracts and pamphlets, and the newly formed League of Universal Brotherhood began advertising itself right from its commencement, aided by its pictorial headed note-paper, which was embellished with an appropriate design. Following the skits and caricatures which had been made of the Mulready envelope, the public were quick to see the possibilities that the new envelopes offered in the way of propaganda and advertising. At first little printed slips of paper had been used to publicize such measures as the Repeal of the Corn Laws, Cheap Bread (with Thanks for Cheap Postage) stuck on to envelopes. Now the entire envelope, sometimes back and front, would be printed with some pictorial cartoon or popular expression of thought.

The League made use of this idea by encouraging the sale to the public of envelopes which were printed with pictorial designs advocating all the causes which it championed. Of the earliest to be published were those in the cause for peace, and the Ocean Penny Post campaign during 1849.

Of the several pamphlets which were published, one in particular was widely circulated. It was only of four pages and very small in size, and was headed simply *An Ocean Penny Postage*, with a sub-title printed in thick capitals WILL IT PAY? This became a catch-phrase of the period.

Shortly after the political upheaval in France in 1848, when Louis Philippe fled to England, Elihu Burritt went to Paris to make preliminary arrangements for holding a Peace Conference, where supporters of the movement for Peace from various countries could all meet one another in conference for the first time. But the grave civil disturbances which took place in Paris during June of that year rendered this impossible. Indeed, at this time there was bad feeling between England and France, and the political situation between the two nations deteriorated. The League once again sponsored an exchange of "friendly addresses" written by private individuals in both French and English towns. A forty-seven page pamphlet published in Paris in 1848 by Elihu Burritt entitled *Adresses Amicales du Peuple Anglais au Peuple Français* was well received and might be considered an early attempt to bring about an "entente cordiale" between the two peoples. Pamphlets called "Olive Leaves" (named after Burritt's Olive Leaf Mission), which were actually tracts against war, were circulated among the working class of Paris, and later were distributed concealed as advertisements in newspapers. The French authorities quickly took steps to suppress these, but there can be no doubt how useful this campaign was in helping to prevent war. Because of the impossibility of holding a Peace Conference in Paris, it was decided to hold the Conference in Brussels. Enthusiastic workers made the preliminary arrangements there, greatly assisted, we are told, by the Belgian Government and local authorities in Brussels, who showed considerable interest in the idea.

The Conference, the first of its kind ever to be held, was a complete

Your faithful friend,

Elihu Burritt.

Plate 14. Elihu Burritt—"The Learned Blacksmith".

Plate 15*a*.
From the *Band
of Hope Review*
of March
1853.

Plate 15*b*. Postage stamps proposed in 1891 for Imperial Penny Postage. Only the name of country and currency denomination would differ.

success. Delegates attended from Great Britain, France, Germany, Holland, and several other countries, and an earnest address was unanimously adopted and sent to all governments of Europe. The English delegation alone numbered 150, reputed to be the largest deputation ever to have crossed the English Channel to attend any Congress or Convention. Burritt relates that on their arrival, after they had grouped themselves for the different hotels, "they proceeded into town, exciting much apparent interest by their arrival".

Thus took place the World's Popular International Peace Congress, brought about by the ardent endeavours of one of America's great philanthropists, the "Learned Blacksmith".

The success of this Peace Congress at Brussels encouraged the movement to organize another in Paris for the next year. In an endeavour to get recognition from Parliament, the League of Universal Brotherhood united with the London Peace Society, the objective being to bring to the notice of Parliament a resolution of Richard Cobden's concerning "stipulated arbitration, or for special treaties between all Christian governments, by which they should pledge themselves to refer to arbitration any question which could not be settled by ordinary negotiation".

Events now moved quickly; a deputation of the Peace movement, which included Burritt, was received by Sir Robert Peel, who, says Burritt, "received us with the utmost courtesy and affable urbanity of a natural gentleman". They took their leave "inspired with the hope that their representations might incline him still more prominently to the policy of peace, feeling sure that any plan he might favour for the abolition of war would commend the considerate attention of the legislators of Europe".

The easing of the political situation in France allowed the next Congress to take place in Paris in October 1849, and, as was the case with the other, the Government helped with the arrangements. It was attended by such notable men as Richard Cobden, Victor Hugo, and Amasa Walker, to name but a few.

There were delegates from the United States and from almost every European country, with about seven hundred from Great Britain, who had been brought over in two special steamers. This Peace Congress of 1849 was referred to as the most remarkable assembly ever convened on the continent of Europe, and was a great personal triumph for Elihu Burritt. *The Times* reported on these Peace meetings somewhat sarcastically, although the Liberal papers of the time were more sympathetic.

In the early part of 1850 Burritt returned to Massachusetts, where he met with a very enthusiastic welcome, and then carried out a highly successful lecture tour of the States on the subject of Peace and the Brotherhood of Man. His fame had preceded him, and by the kindness of everyone along the route, who sincerely appreciated his ideals and his endeavours, he found hospitality everywhere, even his steamship passage on the Ohio River was "on the house".

Burritt returned to England in May that same year and immediately began preparations for a Peace Congress to be held in Frankfurt. This took place in August and, like the others, was held with the same fervent enthusiasm, with an even greater representation of countries. At that time war had already broken out between Schleswig-Holstein and Denmark over the question of the ownership of the territory connecting Denmark and Schleswig—a matter that involved the whole of Germany. By the quick action of the Congress, a settlement of the trouble by arbitration was almost reached, and was about to be negotiated, when Austria entered the conflict by forceful intervention, thereby rendering impossible what might have been a peaceful solution. This incident made a deep impression on the minds of people at the time, for it showed that arbitration was a possible solution to war, although in this instance it was unfortunately unavailing.

While the League's efforts in the cause for peace were actively busy, a plan of campaign for an Ocean Penny Post was also formulated.

This movement was more difficult to get started, for although welcomed by the public, its avowed intention was to improve upon a system which was established by the government of more than one country.

Rowland Hill had been able to state his case for Post Office reform by means of a well-written pamphlet, but the object he was attacking had already been explained and presented to the House of Commons in a most masterly way by Robert Wallace.

Elihu Burritt set himself the task of campaigning for a drastic reduction in an established set of postage rates in use by many different countries, working with nothing more than a zealous ideal to back him. The fact that he was a foreigner, campaigning in a foreign country, in no way perturbed him; his firm belief was that all men were as brothers, and he saw himself on an equal footing with any national in any country. He had a very great respect and deep regard for Great Britain and for all her traditions and institutions, and he had been impressed with the national way of life he had seen for himself during his travels up and down the country. In one of his speeches he mentions:

> One of the plans was to travel on foot through the kingdom, and meet small circles of the labouring classes of the people in small upper rooms, in the different villages through which I passed. And after spending two or three weeks in Manchester and Birmingham, I buckled on my knapsack, and started on my pedestrian tour. I walked about one hundred and fifty miles in this way, holding those social conversational meetings at night . . . but soon I was to address large audiences assembled in public halls. Everywhere I met with the kindest reception, and found devoted and generous friends.

Meanwhile, in the United States agitation was continuing for cheaper postage. In Boston a Cheap Postage Association had been formed which campaigned for a Penny Postage, and in 1848 a pamphlet entitled *Cheap Postage: Remarks and Statistics on the Subject of Cheap Postage and Postal Reform in Great Britain and the United States* was published by Joshua Leavitt.

One of the leading figures concerned with the agitation for cheap postage in the United States was Barnabas Bates, described as a clergyman and a journalist. He was a lively individual, from all accounts, and was one of Burritt's most ardent supporters. It can be said that he was to Elihu Burritt what Henry Cole was to Rowland Hill. It was Barnabas Bates who, about the year 1851, was responsible for having pictorial envelopes published in the United State (Plate 23*b*). Another of Burritt's loyal supporters was his friend, the Hon. Charles Sumner, to whom he wrote frequently, asking him to champion the cause of Ocean Penny Postage in the Senate.

Whether this Cheap Postage Association of Boston (and there was another in New York),[1] together with the agitation that was being

---

[1] During this time Pliny Miles, the secretary of the New York Postal Reform Committee, campaigned zealously for a two cents' uniform rate of postage as

carried out in different parts of the country by supporters of Elihu Burritt, was in any way responsible for cheaper rates coming in force will never be known. But on March 3, 1851, Congress approved a reduction of postage on the inland rates. Up to 3,000 miles the basic rate was to be 3 cents (1½d.) if pre-paid, and 5 cents (2½d.) if not pre-paid. For over 3,000 miles the rates (pre-paid) were doubled, viz., 6 cents (3d.) and unpaid letters were fixed at 12 cents (6d.), but these long-distance rates were again increased in 1855, when pre-payment was made compulsory.

In the spring of 1851, in London, The League of Universal Brotherhood launched two offensives—the first, a campaign for an Ocean Penny Postage, the second, *The Olive Leaf Mission*—a news-paper modelled along the lines of the one Burritt had brought out in the United States when he first became inspired with his Brother-hood of Man ideals. This newspaper was published and printed in many languages and circulated in many countries, payment for its publication in each country being arranged for on very special terms out of sympathy for the aims and ideals expressed in its columns.

Burritt started his campaign for cheap ocean postage by visiting almost all the more important towns in England, Scotland, and Ireland, and addressing large meetings on behalf of the project. At the same time, after holding his Penny Post meetings, he arranged for the ladies in the towns he visited to organize themselves in an association called "The Olive Leaf Society". These two campaigns were thereby carried on side by side, and several of the propaganda envelopes produced for the campaign, which were now appearing in great numbers, published by various firms, incorporated the ideals of both the Ocean Penny Postage project and the Universal Peace and Brotherhood movement.[1] Pictorial notepaper, too, was prepared and used in the campaign. A typical design showed a picture of a ship in full sail, having on her topsail "Ocean Penny Postage", with, underneath:

[1] See Appendix IX, p. 191, and Plates 20–23.

well as for other improvements. Special envelopes with pictorial headings as well as notepaper were used for his campaign. Rowland Hill commented very highly on his efforts.

Fair speed the ship where signal is unfurled
An "Ocean Penny Postage" for the world.

Envelopes showed a mail steamer with a motto on the spread-out foresail: "THE WORLD'S WANT AND SHOULD BE BRITAIN'S BOON—AN OCEAN PENNY POSTAGE". An envelope that served the two campaigns showed an overall design on the back boosting trade between various races, with clasped hands—a white one and a black one, surrounded by little designs symbolical of Commerce. It carried the inscription, "OCEAN POSTAGE ONE PENNY—WOULD LINK IN TRADE AND PEACE—THE BROTHERHOOD OF MAN". Another, embellished with a design showing a sailor standing on the deck of a departing steamer and holding a banner, proclaimed: "BRITAIN! BESTOW THIS BOON AND BE IN BLESSING BLEST—OCEAN PENNY POSTAGE—WILL LINK ALL LANDS WITH THEE IN TRADE AND PEACE".

Burritt, with his fervent admiration for England, looked to England, as being mistress of the seas and the leading power in the world, to show the way and bring this reform about. With his usual unbounded energy, he worked tirelessly and vigorously, and it was not long before his ideas for a cheap overseas postage had caught on not only in England but also in Europe and the United States.

The subject was brought before the Senate of the United States in March 1852 by Mr. Charles Sumner, who introduced it to members by a resolution:

Whereas, the inland postage on a letter for any distance within 3,000 miles is three cents when paid, and five cents if unpaid, while the ocean postage on a similar letter is twenty-four cents, being a burdensome tax amounting, often, to a prohibition of foreign correspondence, —and yet letters can be carried at less cost on sea than on land;

And whereas, by increasing correspondence, and also by bringing into the mails mailable matter now often clandestinely conveyed, cheap ocean postage would become self-supporting;

And whereas, cheap ocean postage would tend to quicken commerce; to promote the intercourse of families and friends separated by the ocean; to multiply the bonds of peace and good-will among men and nations,—and thus, while important to every citizen, it would become

117

the active ally especially of the merchant, the emigrant, and the philanthropist,—therefore,

> *Be it resolved,* That the President of the United States be requested to open negotiations with the European Powers, particularly with the Governments of Great Britain and France, for the establishment of cheap Ocean Postage.

News of this brought great encouragement to Burritt, who wrote of it in his journal, "I now intend to keep the project before the people until the work is accomplished." This he did by intensifying his lectures, by newspaper correspondence, by the circulation of the "Olive Leaflets", as they were called, and in numerous other ways working with unabated perseverance for the fulfilment of the cause so very dear to him.

In company with certain prominent Members of Parliament and other gentlemen, Burritt visited the American Ambassador in London, Mr. Abbott Lawrence, when the question of an alteration in the ocean postal rates between England and the United States was discussed. Mr. Lawrence expressed himself completely in accord with the proposals, saying he would do all in his power to promote the postal reform between the two countries. He considered that an ocean penny postage would take about five years to pay its way, but added that its adoption should not be refused on that account. For, "what," he said, "is $100,000 from the National Treasury against the great blessings which would flow from such a system?"

Burritt now resorted to circulating blank forms to selected people in many places not only in England but also in countries overseas, to be completed in the form of a petition, then returned to him to be sent to Parliament. A good example of the way feeling was aroused by the campaign is expressed in a letter which accompanied the return of one of these petitions. Dated April 1852, from Bytown, Upper Canada (later to develop into the City of Ottawa), the writer says:

Dear Sir:

I have the honour to enclose herewith a memorial from The Town Council of Bytown, to Her Majesty the Queen, praying for the reduction of the Ocean Postage. The obtaining of so desirable a boon can be but a question of time, and from the fact that the pioneers of the

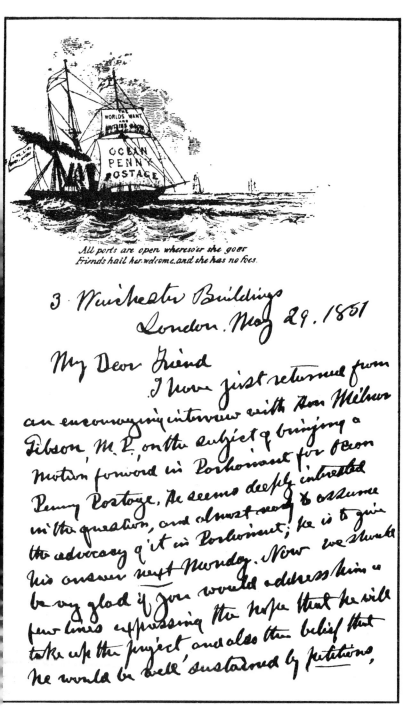

All ports are open wheresoe'er she goes
Friends hail her welcome, and she has no foes.

3 Winchester Buildings
London. May 29. 1851

My Dear Friend
I have just returned from an encouraging interview with Hon Milner Gibson, M.P., on the subject of bringing a motion forward in Parliament for Ocean Penny Postage. He seems deeply interested in the question, and almost ready to assume the advocacy of it in Parliament; he is to give his answer next *Monday*. Now we should be very glad if you would address him a few lines expressing the hope that he will take up the project, and also the belief that he would be well sustained by *petitions*,

Fig. 19. *A letter written by Elihu Burritt during his campaign for an Ocean Penny Postage. (In the collection of G. B. Horton.)*

age have undertaken this reform, there can be but little doubt of its success at an early day. It will be the proudest monument of their philanthropy that has ever been erected, and entitle them to the gratitude of the millions in the old world and the new.

You, sir, have the deserved honor of first giving birth to the scheme, and that you may soon see it realized is the ardent wish of,

Your obedient servant,

R. W. Scott, *Mayor.*

The public's interest was now quickened, for it became aware that the idea of Ocean Penny Postage being brought about was not impossible. The subject was raised in the House of Commons by John Bright, M.P., whose speech was reported in *The Times* of June 26, 1852.

OCEAN PENNY POSTAGE

Mr. Bright said the Right Honourable, the Chancellor of the Exchequer, would be aware that a number of petitions had been presented in favour of the establishment of reduced postage rates between this and foreign countries. The scheme was generally known as an Ocean Penny Postage, and the object of the promoters was that the ocean postage should be reduced to one penny, leaving the rates of internal postage to be fixed at whatever the various countries might think best. The emigrations, now going forward from our shores, made the question one of very much more importance than it had been at any former period, and it was of essential importance that the utmost facilities of communication should be allowed, in order that all which tended to harmony and peace should be maintained as much as possible. The question would be brought before the House in the next Parliament.... There is reason to suppose that the loss of revenue would not be considerable, and, in all probability, in a very short time, the receipts from Ocean Postage would be increased by the enormous increase that would take place in the number of letters transmitted.

Resulting from this, Burritt optimistically wrote in his journal:

Everything tends to the speedy realization of a universal Ocean Penny Postage. Nothing has been lost by the delay which has attended its introduction into Parliament in the shape of a formal motion....

Nearly every day some incident transpires, well calculated to impress upon the public mind the importance and feasibility of this great postal reform. Every day at least one ship freighted with emigrants unmoors from some British port, and spreads its broad wings for Australia, and another for America. And every ship-load of men, women and children thus dislocated from the homes of Great Britain, is a new and pathetic argument in behalf of Ocean Penny Postage. For several months it has been almost the last act of the emigrants to Australia, just before weighing anchor, to sign a petition to Parliament for reduction of Postage.

Although so active with the Penny Post campaign, he still made time to be the controlling force behind the movement for Peace. In 1851, the year of the Great Exhibition, a Peace Congress took place in London, in Exeter Hall, on a scale larger than any of the preceding meetings, attended by prominent men of many countries. The next year, however, the Congress held in Manchester was confronted with the serious state of tension which flared up between France and Great Britain. The League of Universal Brotherhood exerted itself all it could, principally through the medium of written letters and addresses signed by the leading citizens of towns in Britain, and sent to prominent people in French towns; the same idea which had been so successful at the time of the Oregon trouble between Britain and the United States. Whether these letters really helped cannot be known for sure, but the following year saw France and England as allies grouped against their common enemy Russia in the Crimea. This year, 1853, saw the last of the Peace Congresses to take place, in Edinburgh; war had triumphed, in spite of all the talk and good feelings of fellowship promoted during the past few years.

It was during 1853 that an important association was formed, called the Colonial Penny Postage Association, sponsored by the Society of Arts. Its President was Earl Granville, with a Council consisting of thirty-six well-known public men, including some from America, Austria, Prussia, and Spain. Among the names were those of Sir John Lubbock, Baron de Rothschild, Henry Cole, and Elihu Burritt. The Association had a local London committee too, presided over by the Lord Mayor, and local honorary secretaries were appointed all over the United Kingdom, as well as Honorary Corresponding members appointed all over the world, even in such remote places as Batavia, Amoy, and Haiti!

This same year Burritt wrote several letters to the Hon. Charles

Sumner in an effort to increase the agitation for Ocean Penny Postage in the United States. One of these letters[1] in particular reveals the earnestness with which Burritt carried on his campaign. Dated March 11, 1853, from 35 Broad Street Buildings, London, he wrote:

My dear Sumner,

I hope you keep your eye upon what we are doing for Ocean Penny Postage on this side of the water, and that you have not lost an iota of interest in this great reform. I suppose the session of Congress is now at an end, and that you are now in Boston again. But you know that we look to you as the champion of Ocean Penny Postage in the Senate. If I live and my health is continued, I intend to return to America early in next autumn, and take the field in favour of this measure. The British Government has just made a move in the right direction between it and all its colonies. It has proposed to them a uniform rate of 6d, for a letter from any town in the Colonies to any town in the United Kingdom; to be divided in this way—1d for the *inland* service in the mother country, 1d for the colonial inland, and 4d for the ocean transit. This is going just *half* way to Ocean Penny Postage between Great Britain and its colonies. I have just sent an article to the New York Journal of Commerce on the subject, and will you please glance at it, as you will probably find it (in) the reading room you visit, about a couple of days after you receive this note. If you will read it, then I need not repeat here, what it would be otherwise necessary to state. I want earnestly to entreat you to go for nothing short of Ocean *Penny* Postage. Let us nail that to the mast. It will be a glorious reform when carried, and it will associate you with the most grateful recollections in the minds of millions in America. I think we can make a successful agitation in favour of the scheme next season. I hope to speak to many public meetings on the subject in different parts of the Union. Barnabas Bates will co-operate, and other earnest and influential men.

But *you* must be our leader in Congress. You stand committed to this by your own sympathy, and we must rely upon you. If we can establish an Ocean Penny Postage between Great Britain and the United States, it must follow in every other direction. I am sure the British Government will go as far as ours in the matter. So let us make a great movement next season, and the boon will be secured.

I have now presented the subject in almost every large town in the Kingdom; have spoken to 125 public meetings during the last 18 months. Everywhere it has been received with intense sympathy.

[1] Sumner MSS. Harvard College Library.

Ere many months roll around, I hope to see you again face to face. How swiftly these years roll by! It seems but yesterday since I said *good-bye* the last time. Your noble speech on the Fugitive Slave Bill is being reprinted in this country, and I hope will have a large circulation. I should be very happy to receive a few lines from you, whenever you can spare a leisure moment.

Yours ever & faithfully
Elihu Burritt

In another letter written to Sumner dated July 15, 1853, he mentions a new method of propaganda—the setting up of large placards advertising the Ocean Penny Post project, conspicuously placed in fifty of the principal railway stations. Copies of these placards were sent to Sumner, to Barnabas Bates, and to Amasa Walker, in the hope that they would be put up in Boston, where one of the largest public meetings was to take place, in Faneuil Hall.

When the Edinburgh Congress finished, Burritt returned to America, where he campaigned entirely for the Ocean Penny Postage scheme, addressing public meetings in many large cities. He then visited Washington, D.C., where he endeavoured to woo members of Congress on behalf of his postal reform; but other urgent domestic business, in the form of the Nebraska Bill, prevented the proposition from being put forward. So he turned his steps to the Southern States and came back by way of Canada, where he collected several more petitions to present to the British Parliament.

While he was away in America the British Government had decided to lower postal rates to Canada, and to certain other of her colonies, to a basic charge of sixpence per half-ounce letter. It had not been possible to include the United States in the reduction, because the Post Offices of the two countries could not agree upon the division of the ocean postage between them.[1]

The British Post Office had not yet recovered from the experiment of Uniform Penny Postage and was now firmly under the control of Rowland Hill, who had become Secretary of the Post Office in 1854. He, having once been over-optimistic in his own estimations when planning postal reform, was now very cautious in all matters involving Post Office expenditure, and was very much opposed to the

---

[1] It was not until 1868 that the sixpenny rate applied to the United States (G.P.O. Notice No. 43, December 1867).

idea of an Ocean Penny Postage, asserting that it was wrong to compare the cost of transport of letters by sea with the cost by land, as the whole question was based upon a false analogy.

Under Rowland Hill the Post Office was rendering a service to the public which it had never before known. Always the rule was "the public must be accommodated". But he was very strict, and somewhat difficult to get along with, besides being far from popular with Post Office employees, who looked on him as a veritable slave driver. Anthony Trollope, who was one of the Post Office Surveyors, said that he never came upon anyone who so little understood the ways of men as Rowland Hill "unless it was his brother Frederic". His former supporters had tended to drift away from him, probably because Rowland Hill's efforts were now not only for the Post Office improvement but also for the pecuniary improvement of the entire Hill family. An amusing little couplet asked:

> Why is Rowland Hill like a sun-set?
> Because he capped all the little Hills with gold.

His brother Edwin had been in charge of the production of the adhesive postage stamps since their inception in 1840, with Ormonde Hill as assistant. Another brother, Frederic, had been Rowland Hill's assistant since 1851, and Pearson, his son, also held a position in the secretary's office. Pearson Hill invented a machine for post-marking letters during the 1850s.

In 1864 Rowland Hill retired from the Post Office on account of ill-health. Many honours were heaped on him. He was knighted, his salary was changed into a life pension, many honorary degrees were bestowed on him by learned societies, and Parliament gave him a present of a grant for £20,000.[1]

War having broken out in the Crimea, Burritt's philanthropic work in Europe in the cause for Peace was brought to a standstill. He returned home to America, where trouble was shaping itself over the question of freedom and slavery. Burritt advocated Compensated Emancipation, and devoted all his time to writing and lecturing on his views and plans. He travelled thousands of miles. He organized meetings and conventions on the subject, and threw in all his energy into the cause for anti-slavery. The tragedy came when

---

[1] See Appendix X, p. 196.

all his ideals and everything he had worked for were blown sky high, by the outbreak of Civil War between North and South in his own country.

He retired to his farm in New Britain, and for a time relaxed and enjoyed himself pottering about in his fields. But in 1863 he came back to Europe in order to visit old friends and to explore the England he loved so much. Two years later he was invited to become United States Consular Agent in Birmingham, a situation to which he devoted himself with his customary zeal. On a change of government he was recalled home in 1869. Ten years later he died. Although he did not live long enough to see his Ocean Penny Post materialize, at least he had the satisfaction of seeing the establishment of the Universal Postal Union in 1875, when a uniform rate of $2\frac{1}{2}d$. per half ounce came into force, irrespective of distance, between all countries belonging to the Union.

A few years later, on October 1, 1883, Penny Post was established in the United States, when a uniform rate of two cents was introduced on a half-ounce letter.

Elihu Burritt was an idealist, though many might place him among those eccentrics who have energetically advanced new ideas ahead of their time. His theory of Universal Brotherhood was utopian, but was none the less worthy of support; his call for peace proved unavailing, but the very fact that war triumphed showed that such an international peace movement was needed; he did not live to see all his schemes materialize for cheap postage rates between nations, but the campaigns that he launched and sustained with such energy had their effect and are his memorial. If Burritt was an eccentric the world could do with a few more men like him to put forward ideals and influence the conscience of mankind.

CHAPTER 7

Imperial Penny Postage

HENNIKER HEATON, HIS EARLY LIFE IN AUSTRALIA—AS M.P.
FOR CANTERBURY AND A CHAMPION OF POSTAL REFORM—HE
REVIVES THE CAMPAIGN FOR OCEAN PENNY POSTAGE—THE
JUBILEE OF UNIFORM PENNY POSTAGE—IMPERIAL PENNY POS-
TAGE PROCLAIMED

IN 1866 A SMALL pamphlet, printed at Huddersfield and published by Simpkin Marshall and Co., championed a Universal
Penny Postage. It was written by William Hastings "formerly
Agent for Lloyd's, Algiers, and for the Underwriters of Liverpool and
Hamburg". This proposed a postage of one penny per half ounce,
which, said Hastings, should be sufficient for transport (irrespective
of distance), collection, and distribution. He quoted a letter he had
written to the Chancellor of the Exchequer, Mr. Gladstone, setting
forth his plan, but discreetly refrained from printing in full the
reply he received. Suffice it to say that, beyond favouring a penny
postage to all countries, his arguments and explanations were
curious and vague. Another pamphlet published in London in 1871
was entitled *Ocean Penny Postage—Is it Practicable?* This was written
by Frederick Brittain of Sheffield, and set out to prove that the idea
was impracticable; one of his arguments being that in the main the
scheme would benefit only the wealthy merchants, and as they
were well able to afford the prevailing rates of postage, and were
the most regular and constant senders of mail overseas, the Treasury
would, in the long run, lose by it.

We hear no more of William Hastings or of Frederick Brittain,
but their names deserve to be put on record, for it was men such as
these who kept alive the idea of a cheap ocean postage. Some
twenty years after Hastings' pamphlet was published arguments in
favour of such a project were being seriously discussed in the daily

press, and in 1883 the possibility of a cheap ocean postage was again recommended by Mr. Arnold-Forster, in an article which appeared in the *Nineteenth Century*. This question, so ardently campaigned for by Elihu Burritt, was proposed again in 1886, but this time in quite different circumstances.

A young man named Henniker Heaton, born at Rochester, Kent, in 1848, the son of Lt.-Col. John Heaton of Heaton, Lancs., having finished his education at King's College, London, and being adventurous in spirit, went out to Australia to seek his fortune. He began the hard way, accepting the rough conditions of life on the sheep stations, sometimes having to travel hundreds of miles from one station to another. The day came when he quit this sort of work and joined the staff of a newspaper in the town of Parramatta, New South Wales. Here he made his debut in public affairs by acting as the Town Clerk for three months. He switched many times from one paper to another, and for a while edited a paper called *The Penny Post*, little knowing how his life and career were to become so intimately concerned with the name. From Parramatta he moved to Sydney, taking a position on the staff of *The Australian Town and Country Journal*, a paper owned by an influential man named Samuel Bennett, a well-known Australian author and journalist, whose opinion and advice were respected by all, including the Government. Bennett befriended young Henniker Heaton and invited him to his home, where he met and fell in love with his very beautiful daughter, Rose.[1] They married in 1873, making Sydney their home. Henniker Heaton quickly became prominent in the public life of Sydney, and was eventually chosen as a candidate for the New South Wales Parliament. His defeat by a small majority disappointed him greatly, and doubtless this setback was responsible for his decision to return to England. In 1884 he and his family settled in London, where he undertook several temporary appointments connected with Australian interests, but a general election taking place the following year, he successfully contested the seat for Canterbury, and was returned as Conservative Member (see Plate 16).

Like Robert Wallace, the M.P. for Greenock in 1833, Henniker Heaton began his parliamentary career by championing Post Office

---

[1] The original "Rose Lorraine" in the poem of that name, described as one of the three saddest love-poems in the English language.

reform. An oft-repeated anecdote, similar in some respects to the experience of Elihu Burritt, who saw an old lady at the Post Office unable to pay for postage, is related of Henniker Heaton, who, when a young man, saw an old woman in deep distress in a village Post Office. She had just been told that the postage on a letter to Australia was sixpence, and not being able to afford so much, was prevented from writing to her son. Henniker Heaton paid the postage for her, and, as a result, the old lady received £5 from her son, who henceforth wrote home regularly.

In an article written many years later by Henniker Heaton he describes how on one occasion while travelling in Australia he visited a Court house where a young Irishman was being charged with cheating and defrauding Her Britannic Majesty's Postmaster General. At that time newspaper postage to England was one penny, but letters cost sixpence each. Henniker Heaton relates how the young man wrote inside the newspaper:

> My dear Mother,—The long drought has ended in Australia, and I have got a situation at last on Mr. B——'s station at a pound a week. Please God I will send you two pounds at the end of the month. Your Affectionate son, ——.

The newspaper was addressed to his mother in Limerick, Ireland. Henniker Heaton in his account of this says:

> The clever Post-master discovered the message and the man was arrested on Mr. B——'s station for defrauding the Revenue. He was sentenced to three weeks imprisonment and of course the loss of his billet followed. I was unable to interfere with my magisterial friend, but I am afraid that tears started from my eyes when the poor beggar was led to prison.

Doubtless, Henniker Heaton, when living in the wilds of the Australian bush, learned at first hand the excitement and relief of receiving a letter from home, and it may well be that these experiences were responsible for his interest in a cheap postage for overseas letters.

Post Office officials at that time held quite a different view. They had no cause for liking him, for hardly a week passed but Henniker Heaton raised some question in the House concerning the Post Office, a question which, though of benefit to the public, was often

Plate 16. John Henniker Heaton, M.P.

Plate 17a. Cape Colony joined the Imperial Penny Postage system on September 1, 1899.

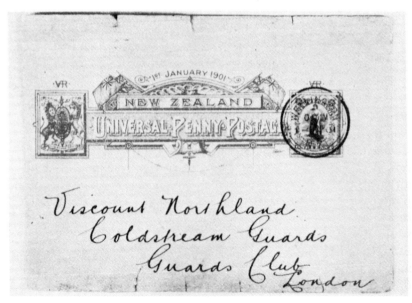

Plate 17b. New Zealand participated with Imperial Penny Postage on January 1, 1901, and issued a special 1d. stamp inscribed "Universal Penny Postage".

an embarrassment to the General Post Office. Scathing criticisms of his postal knowledge frequently appeared in the pages of *St. Martins-Le-Grand*—the Post Office magazine, and in an article concerning his activities with the Post Office the writer implied that Henniker Heaton got into Parliament, not by reason of any ability, but because he was a man of means and leisure, and that he had been advised to take up some special line in Parliament if he wished to keep his seat!

A meeting of the Postal Union had taken place in 1885 when the question of postage rates was studied, for several anomalies existed. For over thirty years our letter rate to Australia and certain other Colonies had remained at sixpence, and it was considered this was too much. In 1886 the rate to all countries of the Postal Union was 2½d., though many exceptions existed, especially to far-away places and to the East. France had decided in 1885 to reduce the rate for all Post Offices under her control to 25 centimes (equal to 2½d.) so that a letter handed in at one of the French Agency Post Offices in Shanghai or Zanzibar, to an address in London, cost the equivalent of 2½d., whereas a similar letter posted through the English Agency in the same places cost 5d. It was indeed galling to know that French people could correspond with our colonies more cheaply than we could! This was the occasion Henniker Heaton chose to make himself heard. On March 30, 1886, he moved a resolution, "That in the opinion of this House the time has now arrived for the Government of this country to open negotiations with other Governments with a view to the establishment of a Universal Penny Postage System." The motion was seconded and an amendment put in by Mr. Hutton, the M.P. for Manchester North, who pointed out that whereas the rate to Canada was only 2½d., to the West Indies it was 4d. Our rate to India was 5d., and to Australia 6d., although the rate from France to India and to the West Indies was only 2½d. It was noticed how Mr. Hutton stole the limelight from Henniker Heaton, for although the credit for reviving the old scheme of a uniform ocean postage certainly went to Henniker Heaton, it was Hutton who drove home the facts; he presented his arguments so convincingly while drawing attention to the glaring discrepancies between English and French rates that, although the motion was defeated, mainly on financial grounds, everyone present was made aware that there were reasons for improvement. Shortly afterwards, when

Hutton was discussing the subject before a Committee of Supply, he moved: "That the interests of this country urgently require that there should be a discontinuance of the charges of higher postage rates from Great Britain to the Colonies than is charged in Continental countries".

He described how a letter from Odessa to the West Indies cost $2\frac{1}{2}d$. while if posted from England, the rate was $4d$. Letters from England to India, Ceylon or China cost $5d$., but from European countries the charge was $2\frac{1}{2}d$. Similarly, newspapers sent to those countries from England cost $1\frac{1}{2}d$., but if sent from Calais, only $\frac{1}{2}d$., and he explained how one business firm saved over £300 a year by sending a clerk across to Calais every Friday with their letters to post from there.

We hear no more of Mr. Hutton, for he was unfortunate in not being re-elected at the next Election. The way was therefore left clear for Henniker Heaton to crusade on his own. Persistently he revived in one way or another in the House of Commons all the questions regarding the discrepancies in postal rates, and his frequent letters to the newspapers on the subject served to keep the public up to date with what was being said. In the meantime France in 1888 reduced the postage to Australia to 25 centimes ($2\frac{1}{2}d$.).

In 1890 the Post Office celebrated fifty years of Uniform Penny Postage.[1] They began with a Jubilee dinner on January 15, when the Postmaster General, the Rt. Hon. H. C. Raikes and nearly three hundred important people, including all the high officials of the Post Office, were present. Speaking at the dinner, the Postmaster General referred to "a question of which we hear a great deal in the newspapers, and something occasionally in the House of Commons— the question of what is called International Penny Postage". After pointing out "the hollowness of the agitation which has been maintained upon this question by simply putting it to the test of the example of Sir Rowland Hill", he decried the whole scheme as being impracticable, for a change was being asked for "which must necessarily diminish the revenue by a great amount and must do it for the sake of the few at the expense of the many".

Forthwith Henniker Heaton replied in a letter to *The Times* of January 28, 1890, and estimated that the adoption of an Imperial Penny Postage plan would cost only £60,000 a year, and would be

[1] See Appendix XI, p. 198.

of great advantage to the Empire. This called forth a reply from Sir Julius Vogel, a prominent colonial statesman and one-time Premier of New Zealand, when he said that it had always been the policy of the Colonies to favour a rapid rather than a cheap postal communication; he pointed out that so long as subsidies were necessary for the maintenance of the mail steamers it was quite impossible for the Colonies to entertain the idea of an ocean penny postage unless the Post Office was to be regarded as a charitable institution for letter writers. He suggested that Henniker Heaton should strive to obtain first a halfpenny rate instead of a penny rate for inland letters, and later, in another letter, he suggested that as the Australian inland rate was twopence it would be better to get that reduced, before trying an ocean penny rate. He remarked that the Australian Colonies themselves showed no desire to adopt an ocean penny rate; in fact, at a recent Conference in Melbourne a proposal to reduce the rate to threepence was rejected in favour of a fourpenny rate!

To all this Henniker Heaton replied that England should and could carry out the scheme, without consulting the Colonies at all, and added that it was well known how the Australian Post Offices were being maintained at a loss, which was the excuse for their opposition to the scheme.

A very real objection to the plan was England's membership of the Universal Postal Union. In order to carry out such a project as an Imperial Penny Postage, it was feared England would be obliged to withdraw from the Union, which would inevitably cause awkward complications.

But the idea was now being discussed freely by many people, and the *Review of Reviews* took up the question and organized a monster petition in aid of a Universal Penny Postage. This, together with the constant publicity given to the scheme by Henniker Heaton in his numerous letters to the Press, doubtless provided the impetus required to get something done. On April 17, 1890, the Chancellor of the Exchequer in his Budget speech proposed the introduction of a $2\frac{1}{2}d$. postage to all the Colonies. He referred to the recommendation of an ocean penny postage, but suggested that as some of the Colonies were opposed to this, it was better not to undertake such a venture.

This measure promptly put a stop to the agitation on behalf of the movement, which would have collapsed and probably vanished for ever but for Henniker Heaton, who continued to ask his usual questions in the House, at the same time suggesting several new measures and drawing attention to some of the postal anomalies that existed. Among the many things he proposed was the possibility of an Agricultural Parcel Post, at one penny a pound; the adoption of a C.O.D. system; the free redirection of letters; and a halfpenny inland postage. This he admitted would absorb all the Post Office surplus, but in defence of his argument he referred to the "conclusions arrived at by the greatest political economists, repeated and never denied in Parliament, viz. that the Post Office should not make a profit, because it is not good policy to do so". A Post Office summing up of this was:

> Does any sane man believe that any British Parliament would be so utterly wanting in common sense as to give up a lucrative source of revenue, raised easily and in a manner which is absolutely unfelt by the people, in order to impose fresh burdens on an overpressed tax-payer? That our latest critic should make such a proposal is enough to stamp him as utterly unpractical.

Although Henniker Heaton was a popular man with the public, and well accepted by the Press, he was very much disliked by the Post Office, who considered him a busybody, always raising questions in the House on matters which they considered he was not qualified to speak about, and they resented the popular reference sometimes bestowed on him as being another Rowland Hill. His continual questioning and remarks on the postal services, though a constant irritation to the Postmaster General, were frequently the cause of amusement to members in the House, where he was popular and respected. For example, it was announced one day mid cheers and laughter that "the Hon. Member for Canterbury will be relieved to hear that henceforth 'mother-in-law' will be counted as one word in a telegram, and an additional grievance to the relationship will thus be removed". To which the Honourable Member for Canterbury replied that he grieved to say his mother-in-law had long since been in a better world, so that he was not in a position to benefit by the change. His efforts for reform had been solely on behalf of Honourable Members not so fortunately situated as himself!

During 1891, a booklet of fifty-six pages entitled *Uniform Imperial*

Postage, An Enquiry and Proposal, by R. J. Beadon, M.A., and published by Cassel at sixpence, appeared under the auspices of the Imperial Federation League. The author's principle was very similar to that of Henniker Heaton, the aim being to establish between England and all her Colonies an Imperial Postage, "cheap, as compared with the system applicable to the outside world, and uniform, because the Empire is a unit, and all the people in it one community". Beadon, however, was against including the United States of America in the scheme, solely because they were not within the Empire (unlike Heaton, who favoured the Imperial penny rate to extend to the United States). He saw little difference in the arguments set forth by Rowland Hill fifty years ago for a uniform penny postage within the British Isles, from the proposals for a uniform rate within the Empire, and suggested the adoption of a postage stamp of suitable Imperial design for the purpose, where only the name of the country and currency denomination required to be changed (see Plate 15*b*). It is curious that Henniker Heaton, who was a member of the Imperial Federation League, resigned from it when this was published.

The pamphlet was well received, and although it did not cause such a sensation as Rowland Hill's famous pamphlet on postal reform, its arguments were seriously considered, and found strong support among many sections of the public. A Postal Committee of the League having been formed, a deputation was sent to the Postmaster General in February 1893, its object being:

> To press upon the Postmaster-General the following points, in view of the probable adoption of the penny rate for overseas letters:
>
> 1. That to whatsoever countries the penny letter-rate may eventually be extended, it shall be first applied to countries within the Empire.
> 2. That a specially designed British Empire penny stamp, with a distinctive mark, for issue in each country of the Empire, be introduced for this particular service.

The spokesman of this deputation was Mr. Arnold-Forster, M.P. for West Belfast, who had first written an article advocating an Imperial Penny Post, ten years previously in 1883.

The Postmaster General, in receiving the deputation, expressed his sympathy with the many objects of the Imperial Federation

League, but made it clear that the Government had come to no decision on the subject, therefore newspaper statements suggesting otherwise were false. He stated that considerable drawbacks stood

Ovȅr· Land·&·Sea·

Fig. 20. *A cartoon from* Ally Sloper's Half Holiday *of December 28, 1892. A popular comic journal of the day.*

in the way, not generally known to the public, and quite apart from difficulties of finance and administration (which, however, were not insurmountable) the principal difficulty concerned the Colonies themselves, especially those of the Australasian colonies. These, in 1891, had joined the Postal Union, under certain terms, and these terms presented a considerable difficulty to the proposals suggested by the League.

A few weeks later, on April 28, a Debate on Imperial Penny Postage took place in Parliament, when a resolution was moved advocating the transmission of all letters from England to all parts of the British Empire for one penny per half-ounce letter. The whole question of an Imperial penny rate was thoroughly explored, and among conclusions reached was one that it would be unfair for the tax-payer to be compelled to bear a loss for the benefit of a limited class. Mr. Gladstone, who took part in the debate, said that Her Majesty's Government had no desire to refuse the proposition, and would be glad to be able to put it into immediate effect, but some important Colonies were averse to it. Moreover, we had covenants with foreign powers which made it impossible for the Government, without breach of honour, to adopt a plan of this description.

A Foreign Office spokesman declared it would not be possible to reduce the postal rates without first obtaining the consent of all parties of the Postal Union, as well as the Colonies themselves, and the legal representatives gave their opinion that Her Majesty's Government was not in a position to establish a lower rate with

134

foreign countries or with colonies already members of the Convention.

It was subsequently agreed to withdraw the resolution. *The Times* on April 29 commented on this:

> In spite of Mr. Gladstone's statement, supported by Mr. Goschen, we contend that there is no foundation in fact for the pretence that honour forbids any change in our postal relations with the colonies. Not only so, but it is open to us if we please to carry our letters to Australia for a penny as we do for soldiers and sailors, even if Australia insists upon charging two pence halfpenny for her letters to us. . . . All this solemn talk about honour and good faith is therefore so much dust thrown in people's eyes. . . . This country can establish an Imperial Penny Post for letters whenever it pleases. . . .

Fig. 21. *A cartoon from the* Sydney Bulletin, *February 18, 1893.*

Henniker Heaton now came forward with an offer, backed by two friends, one an Australian, the other a British capitalist, guaranteeing the Government against any loss that might incur through the establishing of a penny post between all English-speaking peoples, which naturally included the United States. But the offer was rejected!

It was now made quite clear that the Australian Colonies were opposed to the plan, and it was being freely admitted that if England adopted a penny rate to Australasia the colonies there would be entitled to surcharge all letters so stamped as being insufficiently pre-paid.

The effect of this decision on the people of Australia is reflected in the comments of some of the leading Australian newspapers. The *Brisbane Courier* of April 1, 1893, said:

As if the Colonies, Australia or other, could or would have any objection to the mother country sending out letters for a penny, when it was distinctly understood that no reciprocal obligation was involved. . . . If after all this it is asserted the colonies would not consent, the Postmaster General has either credited us with an inane obstinacy, or has forgotten the terms of the proposal made to him. That proposal is that a penny postage should be established from the United Kingdom to the Colonies. There is no *vice versa*. . . . To this arrangement the Postmaster General notwithstanding, no possible objection could be made on behalf of the Colonies. It would not cost them a single farthing.

On May 12, 1893, the *South Australian Register* had this to say:

It is asserted that the Australian people will not consent to England extending her domestic postal rate to her colonies and possessions. We confess frankly that we share Mr. Heaton's opinion that the idea is both presumptuous and absurd. . . .

Obviously, therefore, if Gt. Britain cared to put up with the initial loss of revenue that would result from the taking of the step, that is her business and not ours. The fact that the Australian colonies are not in a position to establish the return service at present should not lead us to stand in the way of the benefits which would undoubtedly result to the people of the United Kingdom and to Australians by the reduction of postage from England to Australia. We have not reached that stage of imbecility yet.

During the Jubilee year of 1897 the occasion was considered by many to be appropriate for the adoption of a Uniform Penny Postage, and Mr. Joseph Chamberlain, the Colonial Secretary, made an important pronouncement at a meeting of the Colonial Prime Ministers in London. He expressed himself in favour of an improved postal service with the Colonies and gave as his opinion that in order for all the countries of the Empire to keep closely together there should be the easiest communication between them, and he believed that Britain should be ready to sacrifice revenue if need be, in order to establish an Imperial Penny Postage. An expression of this sort coming from such an important man raised expectations to a high level, but little more was heard of lower overseas postage rates until later that same year at the Postal Union Congress held in Washington. Here the British delegates tried to get the letter postage rate to all places overseas reduced to twopence per ounce, but the motion was turned down by the representatives of the other nations. An alternative proposal was then made for the adoption of a twopenny rate within a subsidiary union composed of the countries of the British Empire, with the possible inclusion of the United States. While this was being considered, and before all inquiries could be completed, the Canadian Postmaster General, Mr. William Mulock, surprised all members of the Union by announcing that Canada intended to establish a one-ounce letter rate to any part of the Empire for three cents ($1\frac{1}{2}d.$) to start from January 1, 1898.

This announcement on the part of Canada really took "the wind out of the sails" of the British General Post Office. The Postmaster General, the Duke of Norfolk, pointed out how, under the rules of the Postal Union, it was not allowed for one country to reduce its postage to another country without the consent of the latter.

Through the intervention of Joseph Chamberlain, the Colonial Secretary and an ardent Imperialist, the Canadian Government was persuaded to postpone its proposal. In order that matters could be properly settled, an Imperial Postal Conference, the first ever to take place, was announced for June 1898. The Conference, presided over by the Duke of Norfolk, was attended by an imposing number of Postmasters General and delegates from all the Colonies and India, and convened to consider the question of postage rates within the Empire. Attempts were made by Britain, supported by the five Australian delegates, to dissuade Canada from carrying out her drastic proposal, because of the inability of other Colonies to participate, prevented mainly by financial reasons. But the Canadian Postmaster General, supported by the delegates from Cape Colony and Natal, went still further by proposing a penny rate to all places in the Empire willing and able to participate. Britain, with her hand forced by Canada, now abandoned the idea of a twopenny Imperial rate, and after some deliberation accepted the proposal. The outcome of the Conference was to establish the long-awaited Imperial Penny Post which had been demanded for so many years.

It was planned to inaugurate the scheme on the Prince of Wales' birthday (November 9), but this was changed to December 25. According to Mrs. Adrian Porter's biography of her father,[1] the Duke

[1] *The Life and Letters of Sir John Henniker Heaton, Bart*, by Mrs. Adrian Porter (Bodley Head).

of Norfolk visited Queen Victoria to inform her of the initiation of Imperial Penny Postage:

"When does this come into force?" asked Her Majesty.

"We thought of the Prince's birthday," replied the Duke.

Always aware of her supreme authority, the Queen inquired in her most icy tone, "And *what* Prince?"

"The Prince of Peace, ma'am—on Christmas Day," came the quick reply.

Fig. 22. *Imperial Penny Postage, December 25, 1898.* (*Reproduced by permission of* The News of the World.)

Much credit was given to William Mulock for the part he played, for certainly, without his leadership, everything would have turned out otherwise. The Canadian Post Office celebrated the occasion by issuing a special postage stamp, rated at two cents (1*d*.). It depicted a map of the world, with the territories of the British Empire prominently shown in red. Inscribed within a panel was "We hold a vaster Empire than has been", with the date above "Xmas 1898".

For Henniker Heaton, the adoption at last of his pet project was a resounding triumph. *The Times* wrote this tribute to him:

"ADVANCE, AUSTRALIA!"

Australia. "NOT TO-DAY, POSTMAN. IT MAY SUIT THE OTHERS, BUT YOU DON'T LAND HERE FOR A PENNY!"

["Australia will neither send nor receive penny letters."—*Daily Paper.*]

Fig. 23. *A cartoon from* Punch. "Australia will neither send nor receive penny letters."

Henniker Heaton is in reality the Marconi of this new telegraphy of hearts. By bringing the postage of the Empire within the reach of the poorest he has rendered vocal innumerable chords which have long been dumb, and acclaimed the unity of the Empire by the responsive chorus of myriads of gladdened hearts. Christmas is a particularly fitting season for the spread of these glad tidings throughout the Empire, for, after all, the true spirit of Christmas is the out-going of human brotherhood and affection. We do no more than express the sentiments of Englishmen in all parts of the Empire when we offer Mr. Henniker Heaton a hearty Christmas congratulation on the happy inauguration of a really great stroke of Imperial policy.

But for all the praise that came his way, Henniker Heaton was very conscious of the credit due to Mr. Chamberlain, which is reflected in a letter he wrote to one of Mr. Chamberlain's constituents in Birmingham:

When the story of how we won Imperial penny postage comes to be written, it will be found that had it not been for your great representative Mr. Chamberlain we should have had to wait many years for the beneficent reform. I never realized the strength of purpose—his sympathy for the poor, the hardworking people of this country with relations abroad—until the opportunity came for benefiting them by means of cheap postage. The mandarins at St. Martins-le-Grand had the worst half-hour they ever had in their lives in trying to measure swords with the powerful Minister.

Mr. Chamberlain determined that the people should have the boon, and he was ably seconded by my friends Mr. Mulock, P.M.G. of Canada, Sir David Tennant, Agent-General for the Cape of Good Hope together with Sir Walter Peace, Agent-General for Natal.

Cape Colony was unable to participate in the plan until September 1, 1899 (see Plate 17a), having to wait until her contracts with the mail steamers expired, and wanting to know how much would have to be paid under new contracts for the conveyance of the mails to and from England. The Colonies of Australia, NewZealand, and Rhodesia remained out of the scheme.

The turn of the century had many people asking "What next—a Universal Penny Postage?—a halfpenny letter rate?"

CHAPTER 8

Penny Postage to the United States

AGITATION FOR A UNIVERSAL PENNY POSTAGE—ATTEMPTS FOR
A FRANCO-BRITISH PENNY POST—PENNY POSTAGE PROCLAIMED
TO AND FROM THE UNITED STATES

THE NEW CENTURY began auspiciously with New Zealand
joining the Penny Postage group. Indeed, she did more, for
she anticipated events by producing a one-penny postage
stamp inscribed "Universal Penny Postage" (see Plate 17*b*). Henniker Heaton was advised of this in a letter from Sir Joseph Ward,
the Postmaster General of New Zealand, dated August 16, 1900:

> I have much pleasure in informing you that New Zealand will
> introduce Universal Penny Postage from the 1st January 1901, as a
> befitting communication of the New Century and adding another link
> to the chain of Empire.

Specially designed envelopes printed in red and suitably inscribed
"Universal Penny Postage January 1 1901" were available for posting at midnight on December 31 with the new penny stamps, the
postmark applied to them showing the hour as zero.

This adventure on the part of New Zealand was looked upon with
great interest, and with a good deal of speculation, for, as already
explained, by the terms of the Postal Union, the conventional rates
of postage from one Union country to another could not be reduced
without mutual agreement of those countries. New Zealand, by
proclaiming a Universal Penny Postage, appeared to be allowing
foreign countries, that is to say, countries out of the Empire, to
communicate with her at a one-penny letter rate, instead of the 2½*d.*
rate laid down by the Postal Union.

[1] *Life and Letters of Sir John Henniker Heaton, Bart,* by Mrs. Adrian Porter
(Bodley Head).

141

New Zealand emerged from the awkward position in which she had placed herself in a very ingenious manner. Having publicly notified the reduction to all parts of the world, she could not very well withdraw from the announcement. It was arranged, therefore, that all letters pre-paid at the proclaimed Universal Penny Postage rate, and addressed to all countries other than the United Kingdom and countries of the British Empire, should be sorted and stamped with the required additional postage, and then sent on as fully pre-paid letters. The cost of this to the Post Office was merely the cost of the paper and of printing the extra stamps required, apart from the labour involved in the sorting and stamping.

The New Zealand Post Office was censured by the Postal Union for having overstepped the mark, but received many favourable letters from foreign countries expressing their praise and goodwill for the initiative taken in making this move. Certainly New Zealand had taken the first step in announcing to the world what many people confidently expected was sure to happen—the creation of a Universal Penny Postage.

Henniker Heaton was already at work busily organizing an appeal to establish a League for Universal Penny Postage, when an event of importance took place on April 1, 1905. After so many years of ceaseless and untiring work in his campaign for a Penny Post to Australia he received a letter from His Majesty's Postmaster General, Lord Stanley, informing him that a Penny Post was to be established from the United Kingdom to Australia, to commence on April 1. Lord Stanley praised Henniker Heaton for the great part he had taken in helping to bring this about, and said that the credit for it now taking place was largely due to his untiring energy. He concluded by hoping that Henniker Heaton would be able to induce the Commonwealth Post Office to lower its tariff to a penny so that the Imperial Penny Postage would be complete.[1]

Indeed, a remark made by Lord Salisbury some years before contained a greater measure of truth than was realized at the time. He referred to Henniker Heaton as "a supporter of mine

---

[1] The Commonwealth of Australia consists of the six hitherto independent Colonies of New South Wales, Queensland, South Australia, Tasmania, Victoria, and Western Australia, and came into being on January 1, 1901. The Commonwealth joined the Postal Union in 1905.

who is engaged in sticking the Empire together with a penny stamp".

Although he himself was not satisfied with this one-way Penny Post, none the less, it was a great triumph for Henniker Heaton, and congratulations poured in on him from everywhere. A letter from the Lieutenant-Governor and Chief Justice of South Australia, Sir Samuel Way, Bt., recalled the earlier efforts of Elihu Burritt:

My dear Henniker Heaton,

I congratulated you on the 31st March on the accomplishment of Penny Postage from England to Australia, and I am now glad to thank you for your kind thoughtfulness in sending me a letter by the first mail at the penny postage rate.

I have taken an interest in Ocean Penny Postage ever since I heard a lecture at Chatham by Elihu Burritt, the learned blacksmith, in 1850. His scheme, I remember quite well, was really a 3d one.—1d for the ocean transit, and a 1d for the country at each end. Your scheme is really three times as good, and I hope we shall see it accomplished before the year is much older.

Believe me, Yours Sincerely,

S. J. Way

The appeal for a Universal Penny Postage was prepared by Henniker Heaton in the form of a letter and was sent to prominent people everywhere. It emphasized the need for a penny postage rate to be established in all countries of the world "so that when one soul has something to say to another neither colour, nor religion, nor creed, nor diplomacy, nor national antipathy, nor latitude, nor longitude, nor poverty, nor any other barrier shall stand between them". He showed that since Imperial Penny Postage was introduced the outward mails had nearly doubled, and he pointed out how every week our mails for India, Hong Kong, and Australia, all carried at a penny rate, passed through France, yet our letters for France, and brought to Calais by the same boat, were all stamped $2\frac{1}{2}d$. Likewise he asked why a letter to New York should cost $2\frac{1}{2}d$. when a letter carried in the same steamship, and addressed to a place in Canada, many hundreds of miles beyond New York, cost only a penny? These and other arguments he presented in his easy conversational way, and then disclosed that his friend, Sir Joseph Ward, the Postmaster General of New Zealand, intended to move a

143

Resolution for Universal Penny Postage at the next meeting of the Universal Postal Union, to be held the following year in Rome (1906).[1]

At the same time Henniker Heaton was giving great attention to his friends in the United States. He had visited there in 1890, when he first discussed the desirability of a penny post between America and England, with the Honourable John Wanamaker, Postmaster General of the United States. There is no doubt he convinced John Wanamaker of the need for an Anglo-American Penny Post, and in him had an ardent supporter. On every possible occasion he stressed the necessity for a penny post between the two countries.

It was well known to the General Post Office how all sorts of tactics were successfully used by people in getting their letters sent across the Atlantic in either direction for only one penny. A person living in New York would arrange for letters from England to be sent to an address in nearby Canada and then redirected, without any extra charge. Similarly, persons writing to England would have a forwarding address in Canada, for letters to be sent on at the penny rate. For Canada had already established a penny post to the United States. And the General Post Office was powerless to stop these abuses.

By now many prominent people in the United States, such as Mr. Andrew Carnegie, Mr. Theodore Roosevelt, and the former Postmaster General, Mr. John Wanamaker, were taking a keen interest in the plan, so that matters were not allowed to remain still. On July 6, 1906, a deputation of Members of Parliament, with many highly important people, including Senator Longworth of the United States, met the Chancellor of the Exchequer, the Right Hon. Mr. Asquith, and the Postmaster General, the Right Hon. Mr. Sydney Buxton, M.P. Both gentlemen expressed themselves in sympathy with the project, but explained that financial reasons and the probable loss of revenue ruled out the question. Thereupon Henniker Heaton, together with Andrew Carnegie, Sir Edward Sassoon, Lord Blyth, and Mr. Wanamaker, offered to guarantee the Post Office against loss during the first five years of the experiment. But this was not accepted. The following year, after a period of stagnation

[1] Nothing transpired at the Rome Congress, but New Zealand obtained a special vote which allowed her certain privileges alone within the Union.

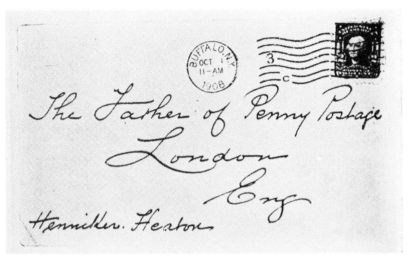

Plate 18a and b. October 1, 1908. Penny Postage to and from the United States of America. Six thousand of the souvenir envelopes illustrated below were carried to the United States by the S.S. *Lusitania*. A similarly designed envelope in blue was published in the United States. (*Courtesy The Bodley Head, Ltd.*)

Plate 19*a* and *b*. The Jubilee envelope of 1890 and the clever caricature by Harry Furniss.

No. 9.

PENNY POSTAGE

TO AND FROM THE

UNITED STATES
OF AMERICA.

ON and after the 1st of October next the postage on letters from the United Kingdom for the United States of America will be one penny per ounce. This uniform rate of 1d. an ounce will supersede the present rates of 2½d. for the first ounce and 1½d. for each additional ounce.

On letters sent in the reverse direction the postage will be 2 cents per ounce instead of the present rates of 5 cents for the first ounce and 3 cents for each additional ounce.

There will be no alteration in the rates of postage on post-cards, printed- and commercial papers, and sample packets passing between the two Countries.

By Command of the Postmaster General.

GENERAL POST OFFICE,
29th September, 1908.

[1081]   Printed for H.M. Stationery Office by W. P. Griffith & Sons Ld., Prujean Square, Old Bailey, E.O.   8/08

Fig. 24.

with nothing more being done about the matter, Mr. George Meyer, the Postmaster General of the United States, sent word to Henniker Heaton expressing his desire to have a penny post established between the two countries. Henniker Heaton forthwith resumed his efforts in the cause, though he was in Australia when he received the message and took the next ship back to England.

In the meantime France was showing sympathetic consideration to the idea of establishing a penny post between France and England. In 1908 the Franco–British Exhibition took place at the White City in London. The guest of honour was the President of France, Monsieur Fallières, and it was thought that this occasion would be a suitable opportunity for the President to meet the Postmaster General and to discuss the chances of a Postal Union between the two countries by setting up a Franco-British Penny Post.

However, the time was not opportune, for discussions had just taken place about the proposed penny post to and from the United States, and to enter into similar discussions with France at the same time might well upset the whole project. These negotiations held between the British and American Postmaster Generals were successful. On June 3, 1908, an announcement was made in the House of Commons:

> The question of Anglo-American Penny Postage (said Mr. Buxton) has been under the consideration of the Postmaster General of the United States and myself. I am glad to be able to announce that I have now received a telegram from Mr. Meyer saying that he is prepared to accept the proposal I made to him for the establishment of Penny Postage between the two countries. Certain arrangements have to be made before the change comes into force, but on and after October 1st next the rate of letter postage to the United States will be the same as that to the Colonies, that is, a penny per ounce throughout the scale, instead of twopence halfpenny as at present. Perhaps I may be allowed to express the confident belief that this reduction in the postal rates between the United Kingdom and the United States will, by greatly increasing the freedom of personal and commercial intercourse, not only further the many interests the two nations have in common, but also strengthen the mutual good feeling which happily exists between them.

In making an announcement to the American public, Mr. Meyer said that the reduced postal rates were limited between Great Britain

Fig. 25. *Penny Postage to and from the United States, October 1, 1908.*

and the United States, the two countries having entered into a special union for the purpose. It was a privilege that could not for the present be extended to other countries of the Postal Union. He believed also that, as a result of this special reduced rate, an improvement in the postal revenue would eventually come about, for the correspondence between the two countries would be enormously increased.

On October 1, 1908, Penny Postage between the two countries came into force (see Plate 18).

The event was given prominent mention in the daily Press. One paper reported:

The first ordinary despatch of letters carried at the reduced rates will take place on Saturday, and the *Lusitania* will be the medium of

147

conveyance. Actually the first mail under the new conditions, however, will be that carried by one of the German liners this morning, but as this takes only letters which are specially addressed the number will not be great. . . . In the mail carried by the *Lusitania* on Saturday will be 6,000 letters enclosed in the souvenir envelopes issued by the Junior Philatelic Society in celebration of the institution of the Anglo-American Penny Post. Nearly 5,000 of them had reached St. Martins-le-Grand yesterday afternoon. The envelope is highly ornamental, and bears the inscription "Penny Postage links the English-speaking peoples of the world". The largest amount of mail matter ever received for despatch to Great Britain in a single day was, says a Reuter's wire, dropped into the New York Post Office boxes at midnight on Wednesday, when the new penny postage rate came into force.

CHAPTER 9

The Passing of the Penny Post

FRANCO-BRITISH PENNY POST CAMPAIGN—OUTBREAK OF THE
GREAT WAR—THE END OF THE PENNY POSTAGE—INCREASED
POSTAL RATES—THE SECOND WORLD WAR—THE CENTENARY
OF PENNY POSTAGE—FURTHER INCREASES IN POSTAGE RATES—
THE END OF THE ANGLO-AMERICAN POSTAL UNION

HENNIKER HEATON NOW gave his attention to the proposed Franco-British Penny Post, which had been so fervently hoped for during the Exhibition year of 1908. In this he was given great help by his friend Lord Blyth, who had been Chairman of the organizing committee of the Franco-British Exhibition in that year. They both went to Paris in 1910 to test public opinion on the question. The Postmaster General of France, various Ministers, and a host of important people gave them a very friendly reception, and everyone expressed themselves in favour of the immediate adoption of a Franco-British Penny Post. But the British Government decided to move cautiously on the question, and backed out of the scheme on the old excuse that the Post Office might be involved in a possible loss of revenue. Actually the reason was deeper than this. In Mrs. Porter's biography of Henniker Heaton she refers to a letter from Colonel Sir Arthur Davidson, the Assistant Secretary to the King, to Henniker Heaton:

> Although, as you say, the question of Penny Postage between France and England is a non-party matter, there are, still, possible international jealousies and difficulties ambushed under such an arrangement; and this being the case, it would be a delicate matter for the King to speak to the Chancellor of the Exchequer on a question affecting France and England only: when other nations, Germany for instance, might wish to retain the present 2½d. rate, and would resent the proposed arrangements as interfering with the International postal balance.

149

This would cause a complication in which it is best that the King should not be included, or have initiated.

You are certainly tireless about postal reform, and have good reason to be gratified with what you have already obtained.

He certainly had cause to be gratified the following year, when on May 1, 1911, Australia at last joined the Imperial Penny Postage Union. The next year Henniker Heaton was created a baronet in reward for his many services.

The outbreak of war in August 1914 put a stop to all thoughts and desires for further improvements in the postal services. Sir John Henniker Heaton was in Carlsbad when war was declared and left for home as soon as was possible. He became seriously ill on the journey, and on reaching the Swiss frontier, doctors advised his removal to hospital. He was taken to Geneva, where he died a few days later and was buried there. He will be remembered not only for his untiring efforts in securing penny postage within the Empire and to the United States but also as being the last of our postal reformers.

Early in the war years it was recommended to impose a halfpenny war tax on all postal packets, but the Post Office rejected the suggestion because it would mean a "tax on communication and the abandonment of the Penny Post which had been maintained for seventy-five years". The penny inland letter rate was retained with the weight limited to an ounce, but on June 2, 1918, Uniform Penny Postage, "one of the great triumphs of peace, succumbed to the demands of war", when the basic charge for letters was raised to $1\frac{1}{2}d$. Its passing was duly commented on in the daily Press. The *Manchester Guardian*, giving an account of the various stages of the Penny Post since Sir Rowland Hill's achievement in 1840, remarked how, but for the war, there might have been a Universal Penny Postage, and expressed the view that perhaps the time would come for "the larger ideal of a penny international exchange".

After the war a real desire was shown for a return to a penny postage, but the Post Office expenses were now too great to warrant such a move. Furthermore, the Post Office was the source of a considerable revenue to the Exchequer, and, to use an expression of Henniker Heaton's when he was championing reform in the 1880s, was the "milch cow of the Treasury".

The inland letter rate was increased to twopence on June 1, 1920, but eventually reduced to 1½d. in May 1922. This inland rate, by reason of the Imperial Penny Postage Act of 1898, and the Agreement made in 1908 with the United States Post Office, still carried a letter to anywhere within the British Empire and to the United States of America.[1]

To mark the centenary of penny postage, it was intended to hold an elaborate celebration on May 6, 1940, but the Second World War prevented this from taking place. Instead, a small exhibition was held in Lancaster House, London, under the auspices of the Royal Philatelic Society, and another exhibition, sponsored by the Postal History Society, took place in Bournemouth.[2]

The postal agreement of 1908 between Great Britain and the United States permitting the inland rate between the two countries remained in force until September 1, 1931, when the United States broke away by increasing its basic rate from two cents to five cents on a letter to Britain. But the General Post Office continued to allow the 2½d. rate on a letter to the United States until October 1, 1957, when Mr. Marples, the new Postmaster General, heavily increased all postage rates and abolished the continuance of the British inland rate to America, thereby completely severing the Agreement of 1908, which had taken Sir John Henniker Heaton so many years of hard and tedious work to achieve.

A penny postage lingered on as the rate for printed matter until June 1, 1951, when that, too, was lost, with the rate increased to 1½d.[3]

Postage rates continue to increase in much the same way as they did in the early part of the nineteenth century. Upon reflection, it should be borne in mind that the Post Office, with its long history, has experienced all this before. After the Napoleonic Wars postage

---

[1] The Imperial Penny Post rate was also increased by all the countries in the Empire, conforming more or less to that of the Mother country. In 1915 Canada was forced to increase to three cents. But in December 1928, the Canadian Premier, W. L. Mackenzie King, announced to His Majesty King George V: "To give enduring expression to the nearness of the relationship of our country to all parts of Your Majesty's Dominions we have, on this Christmas day, restored the penny postage rate on communications from Canada to all parts of the British Empire." Once again, Canada led the way.

[2] See Appendix XII.

[3] The changes in postal rates are given in the Table of Useful Dates, Appendix XIII, pp. 211, 212. The relevant dates are indicated with an asterisk.

rates were increased over and over again, in the same way as they have been since the last two world wars. Today the Post Office no longer contributes to the Treasury, for since 1960 it is allowed to keep its revenue, so that it can expand and improve its services without having to ask the Treasury to sanction money for every payment it makes. Bearing in mind the enormous business undertaken by the Post Office, the service is good, but many people can remember when it was better. The new generation of young people have no experience of the boon of penny postage, so they do not miss what they have never known, and the Post Office, being one of the few government offices in really close touch with the public, is accepted by them as an established necessity.

It should never be forgotten how for over two centuries public-spirited men have striven by individual endeavour, against an opposition backed by officialdom, to achieve a Penny Post reform, as well as other postal reforms. What was frequently regarded as being well nigh impossible was achieved. Now, with ever-rising costs it may well be wondered if a Penny Post plan, even in a modified form, can ever be achieved again.

APPENDIX I

The Penny Post in France

An attempt was made in Paris during 1653 by Monsieur de Vélayer to organize a local penny post, with pre-payment of letters, and collections made from street boxes. It was called "La Petite Poste de Paris", and was allowed to be set up under a Royal decree. A four-page pamphlet describes the advantages it offered and what it set out to do. The following is a brief description and translation:

> To those people wishing to write from one part of Paris to another their letters will be faithfully and carefully delivered, and they will have prompt reply provided that when they write they put on their letters a pre-paid label (un billet qui portera port payé) because money will not be accepted. This label will be put on to the letter or fastened around it, or passed into it, in such a way that the postman can easily see it. Every pre-paid label will have a space for the date to be filled in.

These labels were obtainable at the "Commis General" (the Head Office), and cost one sol each, about one penny. Persons were recommended to buy the labels in quantity, to keep in stock for use as required. Those engaged in legal actions were advised to give them to their lawyers and solicitors; parents were urged to send them to their children at school.

Letters were not to be taken to the post office, but were to be dropped into letter-boxes which were placed in the several "quartiers" of Paris and situated so that no house would be too distant from one. They were to be cleared three times a day—at six o'clock in the morning, at eleven o'clock, and at three in the afternoon, so as to be brought to the office in the Palace Yard.

The Petite Poste did not function for long and fell into disuse. The majority of people who had letters to send also had servants to carry them, and found little need for it. It is said that the letter-boxes were spoiled by having garbage put into them, as well as

153

mice, which ate the letters; whether this was done from malice or
from a perverted sense of humour or through ignorance of what the
boxes were for, we shall never know. Few records exist of Vélayer's
post, so that little is known about it, beyond what is set down in the
pamphlet. It is probable that the labels were in the shape of bands
or wrappers, and that the postman tore them or removed them, this
being equivalent to a "cancellation". This being the case, would
explain their great rarity. A description of one of the port payé letters
is given in Mons. A. de Rothschild's book *Histoire de la Poste aux
Lettres*. In the 1870s this was discussed by the newly founded
French Philatelic Society, when it was decided that the label could
not be considered a postage stamp, but only an historical curiosity.
A delightful reference to the Petite Poste has come down to us in an
advertisement in the form of verses written by the poet Loret, dated
August 16, 1653.

> On va bientôt mettre en pratique,
> Pour la commodité publique,
> Un certain establissement,
> Mais c'est pour Paris seulement,
> De boëtes nombreuses et drues,
> Aux petites et grandes rues,
> Où, par soi-même ou son laquais
> On pourra porter des paquets;
> En dedans, à toute heure, mettre
> Avis, billet, missive ou lettre
> Que des gens commis pour cela
> Feront chercher et prendre là
> Pour, d'une diligence habille,
> Les porter par toute la ville
> A des neveux, à des cousins,
> Qui ne seront pas trop voisins,
> A des gendres, à des beaux-peres,
> A des nonnains, à des commères,
> A Jean, Martin, Guilmain, Lucas,
> A des clercs, à des avocats,
> A des marchands, à des marchandes,
> A des galants, à des galantes,

A des amis, à des agents,
Bref à toutes sortes de gens.
Ceux qui n'ont suivants, ni suivantes,
Ni de valets, ni de servantes
Seront ainsi fort soulagez
Ayant des amis loin logez.
Outre plus, je dis et j'annonce,
Qu'en cas qu'il faille avoir réponce
On l'aura par mesme moyen.
Et, si l'on veut savoir combien
Coûtera le port d'une lettre,
Chose qu'il ne faut pas obmettre
Afin que nul n'y soit trompé,
Ce ne sera qu'un sou tapé.

The French Postal authorities were very interested in the British postal reforms of 1840 and sent over an observer to report on the uniform Penny Postage plan. They considered a uniform rate of a penny too ambitious for their purpose, and feared too great a fall in revenue. Cautiously they waited for nine years before introducing a uniform rate of twenty centimes (2d.) on January 1, 1849. Postage stamps were also issued, and were compulsory for pre-paid letters.

The French public had to wait many years before getting a penny post. The much needed reform in the French Post Office for a reduction in postage to a uniform rate of ten centimes (1d.) received legislative sanction in 1906. While other countries in Europe had already copied Britain's example and had adopted a penny post, the people of France did not have this privilege; their basic inland rate was fifteen centimes ($1\frac{1}{2}d.$). A long-continued agitation undertaken from Paris at last found the best way of drawing attention to the cause—by means of the picture postcard.

The Paris daily newspaper, Le Matin, which strongly championed the cause, issued pictorial postcards showing the postage stamps of several European countries corresponding to a one-penny rate. These postcards were primarily intended to be sent to the president of the Chamber of Deputies to call his attention to the widespread dissatisfaction with the existing high postal rates. The postcards showed all the stamps printed in red—the colour selected by the

Universal Postal Union for the inland one-penny rate for a minimum of 20 grammes, and depicted the postage stamps of Germany, Austria, Hungary, Belgium, Great Britain, Holland, Luxemburg, and Switzerland. A space was left, labelled "France—15 centimes, 15 grammes". These postcards are now much sought after.

Correspondence Disputing the Invention of the Penny Post

The following printed letter signed by Robert Murray and dated July 2, 1680, is from the Harleian MSS., Bagford Collection, 5954 in the British Museum, and is the only known copy. The extract of Chamberlen's letter that follows it is printed on the same sheet of paper.

Mr.

The Undue Practises, and Scandalous Reflections of Mr. William Dockwra, which he hath expressed, as well by Letters dispersed in and about the City, as otherwise, concerning my undertaking to Convey Letters and Pacquets according to my first Proposal, hath put me upon the necessity of this Vindication: It would be troublesom to mention each particular. In short, the Sum of all is issuable in this; He that dares not, or will not Refer his Cause to the Judgement of Discreet and Indifferent Men, is (upon good Reason) suspected to be in the wrong; Mr. Dockwra hath often been requested by Me to Refer the Matter in Difference between Us, but hath always refus'd it: If he should be so Obstinate as to deny this, I canu (*sic*) make out the Truth of it by divers Credible Witnesses.

It is very well known that I am the Original Contriver, and Author of this way of Conveying Letters and Pacquets, and the first that ever proposed the doing of it; and that upon my Discovery thereof to Mr. Dockwra, He and I entered upon the Performance of it as Partners together; Besides, the same was acknowledg'd by him in the Presence of Doctor Hugh Chamberlain, before the Right Honourable the present Lord Mayor: I do not therefore (as he alledges) set up a new Peny Post, but only continue my own Invention and Method before-practised while Mr. Dockwra and I were together, which I do as my own Right, and to secure my self against his Usurpation and Oppression; I never yet insisting on any other Tearms than what I ought to have had by the Original Agreement between Us, from which he hath most Injuriously departed, with a Design to Ingross all the Power and Interest in it into his own Hands. Now Matters being duly Consider'd, I am so confident of Your Affection to Common Right and Justice, that You will not Desert the Innocent by any Artifice of Mr. Dockwra, from whom I only endeavour to deliver my self this way, having in all things approv'd my self Just to Him.

I am, Your Humble Servant,
Rob. Murray

An Extract of a Letter from D.H.C. to Mr. Dockwra, left to me to deliver if I thought fit. The Original I have ready to produce.

What can justify your telling me (after my Name had been tossed about the Town, my Personal Attendance, Time, Interest, Advice, and Reducing your Precipitate Undertakings into some Orderly Method,) that Mr. —— failing, under whom I claimed* my further pretence to any Share, was void; Nor would you then so much as promise me 500 l. out of the Profits. When I offer'd you to quit all Claim; And yet (out of respect to the Publick Advantage by the Design, and my mistaken Opinion of Your Worth) to give you all reasonable Assistance both by Person and Pen: But above all, what can justifie your barbarous exclusion of Mr. Murray, who was the Original Projector, and the Laborious Manager of the whole Design? Was not He exempted from any Charge in the promoting the Business? was He by Articles oblig'd to bring in another Partner? was it not His being Projector of it, Consideration enough? and the only Consideration You voluntarily consented to, and frequently confirm'd, what mov'd You to joyn in Articles with Him? which (though never Executed) oblige the Consciences of Honest Men, as much as Law does Knaves upon Seal'd and Deliver'd Deeds; For that which obligeth is Consent exprest by Words, the Writing is but Evidence of these Words. I have not a Memory to treasure up particulars; But these may be sufficient to rouse up an honest Mind to wipe off those Suspitions, if they be not just Accusations: from which I should be glad if you can vindicate your self, and still deserve the Friendship heretofore readily admitted, By

Sir,
Your injur'd Acquaintance,

July 2d. 1680   H. CHAMBERLEN.

* Not expected till they had cleared to themselves 5000 l.

A letter from William Dockwra which appeared in the *Daily Courant*, No. 229, January 11, 1703:

Whereas a malicious false Report has been industriously spread, That one Robert Murray was the first Inventor of the Penny Post, and that he has been in articles with me William Dockwra, and wrong'd and hardly used: The World is desired to take notice, That as to the first Pretence it is utterly false, for Dr. Chamberlen, one Henry Nevill Payne, and others, pretended themselves the first Inventors; And after I had actually set up the Office, one Mr. Foxley came and shew'd me a scheme of his concerning a Penny Post, which he had offer'd to Sir John Bennet Post-Master General eight years before I ever knew Murray, but that was rejected as impracticable, as indeed were all the rest of their Notions; nor ever was it by any of them, or any other Person whatsoever, put into any Method to make it practicable, till at my sole Charge and Hazard I begun it in the Year 1680.

As to the Articles they were sacredly kept on my part, but never perform'd by Murray, to my great Loss and Damage, as by the very Articles themselves will evidently appear; and I am ready at any time to demonstrate, it is so far from having one Shilling due to him, or using him in any way hardly, That on the contrary, in Compassion in his distressed Condition, I have often bayl'd him, to keep him out of Prison, and redeem'd him from thence, lent him several Sums of Money, which he never took care to pay again; and to this day I have Notes and Bonds to produce, that he owes me more than One hundred and fifty Pounds: So that these most unjust and ungratefull Allegations in Murray, are at this time reviv'd to be made use of, as malicious Reflections to lessen my Service to this City, and to stain my Reputation and Integrity thereby, to hinder my Fellow-Citizens kindness upon this Election for Chamberlain, which I hope will make no Impression, since I do affirm myself to be the first that ever put the Penny Post into practice, at a vast Expence and great Loss to me and my Family.

William Dockwra

An Account of the Penny Post from
The Present State of London, *1681*

The following account of the Penny Post is taken from *The Present State of London*, by Thomas De Laune, published in 1681. It is the most comprehensive contemporary description.

Of the PENNY-POST

This Ingenious *Undertaking* being so extraordinary useful in the facilitating of Commerce and mutual Correspondence, and consequently very serviceable to *Traders*, &c., shall be briefly handled; and, I hope, that what proceeds from me, who am no interested Person, will be resented Candidly, and Examined, as to the Argumentative part, according to the Solidity and Strength of the Reasons produced.

I have heard this Undertaking disparaged by some Censorious Persons, and have examined the Reasons, with the quality of the Objectors, and have found it all along opposed by none but the Ignorant, or such as preferred some particular Ends, before Publick Utility. To my knowledge I never saw nor corresponded directly nor indirectly with any of the Undertakers, till being very desirous to insert this Affair of the *Penny-Post* in this Book for Publick Information, I made an Address to one of the Gentlemen concern'd, who Courteously supply'd me with some particular Informations which I wanted, and for which I am beholding to him. This I speak, to satisfie the Objectors that I do voluntarily, and not by any inducement of theirs mention this Affair, which, in my opinion, is so far from being a prejudice, that the City, as well as the whole Nation, is beholding to them for their Ingenious Contrivance, and their Constancy and Generosity in minding the Publick Good so much as they have done; for 'tis certain that they have been at very great Expence to hold it up, under the Discouragements that some Persons have

160

thrown upon them, and the necessary Charge to support it is yet very considerable. But to be more particular:

1. I will give some Hints of what this Undertaking is in Point of Practice.
2. Its general and particular Usefulness.
3. I will consider an Objection or two.

1. What I can say of this Undertaking in Point of Practice, is briefly what follows, only I would premise a few words as my opinion, and the opinion of impartial Persons of my acquaintance, as to the thing in general.

This useful Invention is little more than a year old, being begun in *April*, 1680. The chief Undertaker that introduc'd it into Practice, is one Mr. *William Dockwra* Merchant, a Native and Citizen of *London*, formerly one of His Majesties *Sub-Searchers* in the Custom-House of *London*, as in the List of those Officers appears. A Person, whose approved Reputation for Industry and Fidelity was well known to all for above ten years in that Office: And to whom the Publick is obliged, he having, with his Partners, spent much time, and a great Sum of money, to bring this Undertaking on foot, wherein they encounter'd with no small Difficulties, not only by *Affronts* and *Indignities* from the *Vulgar* sort, who seldom weigh any Publick or Generous Designs, but at the *Beam* of Little, Selfish, By-Ends, but also by more dangerous Attaques; for there have been Attempts made, by some Persons, to persuade his Royal Highness the Duke of *York*, that it intrench'd upon the *General Post-Office*, and damnifi'd it; whereupon many Actions were brought, and a chargeable Suit of Law follow'd: But, questionless, the Duke is better inform'd now; for it is most certain, that this does much further the Revenue of the *Grand Post-Office*, and is an universal Benefit to all the Inhabitants of these Parts; so that whoever goes about to deprive the City of so useful a thing, deserves no thanks from the Duke, nor any Body else, but to be Noted as an *Enemy to Publick and Ingenious Inventions*.

It is with all Humility submitted to the Consideration of all worthy Citizens that happen to peruse this small Tract, that it becomes not the Honour of the City to suffer any of its *Ingenious Natives*, especially Persons who have lived and do live in good *Fashion* and *Repute*, to sink under the carrying on of an Undertaking so advantageous not only to the Publick, but also to private Persons, since their industrious Service to their Generation deserves encouragement from their Fellow-Citizens, and all others, *viz.*

(1) To discountenance petty Persons that would, for the profit of running of Errands, rob the Community (if they could) of this more than ordinary convenience for safe, cheap, and necessary Dispatches.

(2) To reject any INTRUDER that may attempt to set up another *Penny-Post*; because, if the thing be hereafter profitable, all the Reason and Equity in the world will plead for the Inventors, *viz.* that they ought to reap the Benefit. And it is a Note of Consideration, that Mr. *Dockwra* has a numerous Family of eight young Children; who being forsaken by some others soon after it began, and left to shift for himself, carried on this Undertaking singly, for above half a year at his own proper charge and hazard, against all the Difficulties, Oppositions and Discouragements that attended it, though now he hath several Citizens in partnership with him. But I am truly informed, that the Income does not yet amount to three-fourths of the necessary Charge to support it; therefore I am persuaded that this Honourable City will employ the *Inventers*, rather than an Invader, if ever such should be; And that 'tis much below such a Prince as his Royal Highness is, to desire the Ruine of such a Family.

I am the more large upon this Particular, because it would be a general Discouragement to the Contrivers of useful and profitable Inventions, if others should be encouraged to reap the Crop of what they with so much charge and labor have sown.

This Penny-Post is thus Managed.

The Principal Office to which all Accompts, &c. are daily transmitted, is in *Lyme-street*, at the Dwelling-house of the said Mr. *Dockwra*, formerly the Mansion-house of Sir *Robert Abdy* Knt.

There are seven *Sorting-houses*, proper to the seven *Precincts*, into which the Undertakers have divided *London*, *Westminster*, and the Suburbs, situated at equal distances, for the better maintenance of mutual Correspondence.

There are about 4 or 500 Receiving-houses to take in Letters, where the Messengers call every hour, and convey them as directed;

as also Post-Letters, the writing of which are much increased by this Accommodation, being carefully convey'd by them to the General Post-Office in *Lombard-street*.

There are a great Number of Clerks and poor Citizens daily employed, as Messengers, to Collect, Sort, Enter, Stamp and Deliver all Letters, every Person entertained giving Fifty pounds security, by Bond, for his Fidelity; and is to be subject to the Rules and Orders, from time to time, given by the Undertakers, who oblige themselves to make good anything deliver'd to their Messengers under the value of Ten pounds, if Sealed up, and the Contents Endorsed; And these Messengers have their Wages duly paid them every Saturday night.

By these are convey'd Letters and Parcels, not exceeding One Pound Weight, nor Ten Pound in Value, to and from all Parts at seasonable times, *viz.* of the Cities of *London* and *Westminster*, *Southwark*, *Redriff*, *Wapping*, *Ratcliff*, *Lyme-house*, *Stepney*, *Poplar*, and *Blackwall*, and all other places within the weekly Bills of Mortality, as also to the four Towns of *Hackney*, *Islington*, *South-Newington-Butts* and *Lambeth*, but to no other Towns, and the Letters to be left only at the Receiving-houses of those four Towns, for the said four Towns; but if brought home to their Houses, a Penny more in those Towns; nor any Letter to be deliver'd to them in the Street, but at the Receiving-houses.

They do now use *Stamps* to mark the hour of the Day on all Letters when sent out from their Office to be deliver'd, by which all Persons are to expect their Letters within one hour, (little more or less, from the time marked thereon, excepting such Letters as are to be convey'd to the Out-Towns, and Remotest parts, which will be longer) by which the cause of delay of Letters may be easily discern'd, *viz.* whether it be really in the Office, or their own Servants, (or others) with whom Letters are left.

The Marks they make use of for this purpose, are these:

Fig. 26.

Of which the First, signifies Eight in the Morning, the Last, Four in the Afternoon, and the Middlemost, is the Letter of the Chief Office in *Lyme-street*, each Office having its proper Letter, and an Acknowledgement that the *Penny-Post* is paid, to prevent the giving of anything at the Delivery.

All Persons are desired not to leave any Town-Letters after Six of the Clock in the Winter, and Seven in the Summer on Saturday Nights, because the many poor men employ'd, may have a little time to provide for their Families against the Lords-day, having no leisure all the week besides.

Upon three days at *Christmas*, two days in *Easter* and *Whitsontide*, and upon the 30 of *January*, the *Penny-Post* does not go.

To the most Remote places Letters go four or five times of the day, to other places six or eight times of the day. To Inns of Court, and places of business in Town, especially in Term or Parliament-time, 10 or 12 times of the day. For better information of People where the Receiving-houses are, there are great Numbers of Printed Tickets dispersed from time to time amongst the Neighborhood, and Advertisements in the Publick Intelligences, which all concern'd may take Notice of, so that any body may be by the Neighborhood immediately inform'd where a Receiving-house is. Carriers and Stage-Coach Letters are to have Two-pence inclosed to each Carrier or Coachman, because they often reject them for want of money; Hundreds of such being return'd, which any Inquirer may have again upon notice, for they lie Alphabetically disposed of in the chief Office for that end.

On all Post-Nights due Care is taken to call for, and convey to the General Post-house in *Lombard-street* all Post-Letters, whether Foreign or Inland, left in any of the *Penny-Post* Receiving-houses, at or before Nine of the Clock at Night. And I could wish, for Encouragement of the Undertakers, that all Persons would so far contribute to the continuance of this useful Design, as to send their Post-Letters by this Conveyance to the Post-Office in *Lombard-Street*, which they do not Convey by themselves, or Servants.

If any Post-Letters be left without Money that should pay beforehand, they will be Returned to the Office, therefore such as send Money, are to indorse the Postage-money upon their Letters.

Such as inclose Money in Town-Letters, are to Indorse the true

Sum on the Outside, and to tye fast and seal up, under a plain Impression, all Parcels, which may be one way to prevent Disputes, in case anything be lost. The Undertakers will not answer for any Contents unseen, unless sealed fast, and the Value Indorsed plain to be Read.

2. *Some brief Hints of the Usefulness of this Office.*

1. In and near this great and famous *Emporium*, is the usual Residence of our Kings, the High Court of Parliament, the fixed Seats of all the Courts of Judicature, and in it is managed a vast Trade, as was shew'd in the *Chapter* that Treats of it; now a cheap, frequent, and safe way of Correspondence, is very advantageous for all that are concerned in Commerce, or Business.

The principal Trade of *London* depends upon Navigation, and therefore the City and Suburbs are situate along the River of *Thames*, extending in length, as was shew'd, pag. 5, from *Lyme-house* to the end of *Tuttle-street* 7500 Geometrical Paces, that is seven Miles and an half; and from the end of *Blackman-street*, to the end of *St. Leonard Shoreditch*, 2500 Paces in Breadth, that is two miles; and the whole Circumference (as by Demonstration can be made apparent) is above 20 Miles, taking in all the Contiguous Suburbs and *Westminster*, so that it is the longest, if not the greatest and most populous City in *Christendom*. This extraordinary Length, though it adds to its Splendor and Beauty, yet it renders speedy Communication and Intercourse in Business very uneasie, and much more troublesom, than in such great Cities as *Paris*, which is almost of an orbicular Form. Now to keep up a necessary Correspondence, the way formerly used, was to hire *Porters* at Excessive Rates to go on Errands, and to send Servants or Apprentices, who, in the mean while, lost that time that should be spent to learn their Trades, and benefit their Masters, and would often loyter, and get vicious habits, and evil company, &c. (when they need not) to their own and Masters hurt; or else such as could not spare the Porter so much money, nor kept Servants, (as some poor Artificers and Labourers) have been forced to sweat and toil, and leave their work, for, it may be, half the day, to do that which now they may perform at the easie rate of a Penny.

But now all these Inconveniences are remedied by the *Penny-Post* with great Safety and Celerity, for which the Contrivers really deserve the Thanks of all who reap benefit by it; and I may be bold to say, that all the Inhabitants in general, and their Fellow-Citizens in particular, are already very sensible of the great Convenience thereof: For, among the innumerable Benefits of this *Penny-Post*, which, for brevity we omit, Friends may converse with Friends, at any distance; Merchants, Shop-keepers and Tradesmen with their Customers, or such as deal with them; Clients may consult with Lawyers; Patients with Doctors; Poor Prisoners with Creditors, or Benefactors; and all Bills dispersed for Publication of any Concern; All Summons or Tickets conveyed; all Entries of Brewers to the Excise-Office; and many more, for *One Penny*.

3. *The Objections I have heard of, are,*

1. From some sort of *Porters*, viz. that it hinders their Livelihood.

Answ. (1.) 'Tis certain that this is a mistake, for their Livelihood never depended upon going on Errands, their Business being other laborious Work, and carrying of Burdens, &c. But some of the Free-Porters are now in the service of the Undertaking.

(2.) Most Business dispatcht by this Undertaking, was formerly either not done at all, or performed by other hands, to save Charges, (Porters Rates being so dear) and Persons themselves, or their Servants, went on their own Errands.

(3.) If the Porters, who are an inconsiderable Number, in respect of the whole Inhabitants of this great City, should suffer some small loss of Petty Employ by it, yet vast Numbers of poor People, and others, are exceedingly eased and benefitted thereby, which deserve as much, or more pity, than Porters: And a general and useful Undertaking, should not in Equity or Prudence be discountenanced, for the peculiar advantage of some few, any more than all the Pipes or Water-Conduits of the City should be destroyed, meerly for the Accommodation of Tankard-Bearers; Printing suppressed, to accommodate Writing Clerks; Guns, for Fletchers; Navigable Rivers, for Carriers; and the Trade of Jack-smiths, for Turnspits, &c. Nor have Porters any Authority to monopolize to themselves the Delivery of Letters, it being by Law free for any Person to use what Conveyance they think good for their Letters, within or without the Freedom. And Coach-men, Car-men, Water-men, &c. may as well be put out of their Callings, as the Undertakers disturb'd in this Concern, because then the Porters may have more Burdens to carry. Neither is any prohibited or restrained by this Undertaking, but they may still employ a Porter if they please, so that this Objection is causeless, and is level'd against the whole Body of Inhabitants, as well as the Undertakers in particular.

2. Others Alledge, That their Letters are not speedily answered, and therefore say they miscarry.

Answ. That may be, because the Party is not at home, and his Servants do not produce his Letter as he ought, though punctually left by the *Penny-Post-Messenger* (this I have very often known to be my own Case, and some of my Friends.) Or the Party may not be at leisure, or not willing to write, or removed, or would pretend he received it not, when Dun'd for money, which he cannot, or will not pay. And indeed I am also inform'd, that abundance of Letters are so ill superscribed, or uncertainly directed, when frequently the particular Trade of the Party, the Sign, or what Noted Place is near, are omitted, that it is impossible to deliver such, which is the fault of the Senders, and not of the Office.

To conclude this Subject. The Reader may expect hereafter a small Tract by it self, Printed for the Undertakers of the *Penny-Post*. What I have here inserted being briefly Remarkt, as my own Notions, concerning so laudable a Design, by way of *Specimen*, and as a thing suitable to my present Work.

Post Office Bellmen

Bellmen were a part of the London street scene during Dockwra's time, for he mentions them in one of his handbills, ". . . yet some persons through neglect of this useful Contrivance, have preferred the Bell-man and other obscure persons, rather than the use of the Penny Post . . .". At this time they were most likely "cryers" of news, or were hired to announce some bargain or "special line" for sale in the shops, and let themselves be hired for running on errands and carrying messages.

Early mention of bellmen in connection with letter-carrying is given in two letters written from London in 1701 to Mr. Thomas Coke. The first, dated in January, is from his wife: "the bell rings for my letter, and makes me lose the happiness of fancying I am talking with my dear . . ." The second, written by Thomas Jennens and dated July 15, concludes, "the bell rings for the letters; my wife's and my service to Lady Mary and your sisters . . .". From this mention of the bell, it is fair to suppose that it was a postman's bell, rung by a messenger going from street to street to collect letters, and not merely a household bell, used like a dinner bell, to summon the time for letters to go to the post. This being so, it is easy to perceive how, a few years later, in 1709, Charles Povey decided to employ bellmen in the streets for the collection of letters, when he set up his Half-Penny Carriage.

The idea was considered a useful one, and the bell-postmen could not have been altogether in general use, for, when the Government suppressed his Half-Penny Carriage for letters, they adopted the idea of bell-postmen for the collection of letters, and for more than a century they became one of the familiar noises of the London streets. In a little book entitled *The Picture of London for 1805*, it is stated:

> Houses, or boxes, for receiving letters before four o'clock at the
> West-end of the town, and five o'clock in the City, are open in every

part of the metropolis; and after that hour bellmen collect the letters during another hour, receiving a fee of one penny for each letter.

When the General Post Office abolished bell-ringing in London the *Illustrated London News* had this to say, on June 27, 1846:

> We have just lost another of what poor Thomas Hood called "those evening bells". The Postmaster-General having issued his fiat for the abolition of "ringing Bells" by the Letter-Carriers, the last bell was rung in the City on Wednesday last. The "ringing" will be entirely discontinued after the 5th of next month; . . .

Bell-ringing lingered on for a few more years in other places in the kingdom, although there is little documentary evidence of this. An inquiry made during the 1890s among Post Office employees in the cities of Edinburgh, Glasgow, Manchester, and Liverpool failed to produce any knowledge of bell-ringing within their lifetime. But in Dublin it is recorded that bell-ringing came to an end in June 1859. The reason for its survival in so large a city as Dublin was because the letter-boxes at the receiving houses and the chief office closed two hours before the despatch of the night mail. When they closed, bellmen commenced their rounds, ringing for this night mail despatch only. They had to bring their evening's collection to the chief office one hour before the mail went out. For this each bellman received a personal fee of one penny a letter, and one halfpenny for every newspaper, paid by the sender.

Doubtless the introduction of street letter-boxes in 1855, with frequent collections, made the bellman's job obsolete. But he was heard of in Leamington as late as 1866. Probably the last mention of a bellman belongs to Edward Capern, the postman poet, who died in June 1894, at the age of seventy-six. He expressed a wish that his old postman's bell—the one he used so long as a letter-carrier between Bideford and Buckland Brewer—should be buried with him. The bell can be seen today inserted into the Dartmoor granite gravestone which stands to his memory in the churchyard at Heanton Punchardon, Braunton, Devon, where he lies buried.

APPENDIX V

An Account of the Penny Post

(From *Vade Mecum*, 1692 by John Playford)

Whereas by an Order from the post-Master General, bearing Date the 11th of *March*, 1684/5; all Carriers, Stage-Coaches, Higlers, and Drivers of Pack-Horses, are forbidden to Carry, or Re-carry any Letter, or Pacquets of Letters, except what concerns their Packs, upon the Penalties therein exprest; Therefore for the better Accommodation of all Persons in their Correspondency, there are Foot-Posts setled for the Collecting and delivering of all Letters, as well for the *General Post-Office*, as others, to these Towns round *London*, brancht out from the Six Offices; as followeth; *viz.*

From the Office for WESTMINSTER-Precinct, in Dukes-Court, near St. Martin's Church, to

CHELSEY	
BLACKLANDS	
EARLS-COURT	
SANDY-END	
THE GROVE	
PARSONS-GREEN	
WALLHAM-GREEN	
NORTH-END	Twice a day; at Eight in the Morning, and Two in the Afternoon.
FULHAM	
HAMMERSMITH	
CHISWICK	
STRAN ON THE GREEN	
TURNHAM-GREEN	
OLD-BRANFORD	
NEW-BRANFORD	
THISTLEWORTH	
TWITTENHAM	

KNIGHTS-BRIDGE BROMPTON THE GOWER KENSINGTON SHEPHERDS-BUSH WHITTON TEDDINGTON MOSELEY WALTON WEYBRIDGE	Twice a day; at Eight in the Morning, and Two in the Afternoon.
EAST-ACTON ACTON-TOWN LITTLE EILING GREAT EILING HANWELL SOUTHALL HAYES HILLENDON UXBRIDGE DENHAM GERRARD-CROSS HEDGERLEY BOULSTROUD BEAKONSFIELD NORTHALL PERRYSFIELD GANFORD-TOWN and GREEN HARROW O'TH' HILL PINNER RICKMANSWORTH	Once a day; at Eight in the Morning.

From the Office for the TEMPLE-Precinct, in Chichester-Rents, near Lincolns-Inn

PANKRIDG KENTISH-TOWN HAMPSTEAD HIGHGATE	Twice a day; at Eight in the Morning, and Three in the Afternoon.

HENDON	
HORNLY	
MUZZLEHILL	Once a day; at Eight in the
CONYHATCH	Morning.
WHETSTON	
TOTTERIDGE	

From the Office for St. PAUL'S-Precinct, at the Royal Bagnio-
Coffee-House in Newgate-Street, to

ISLINGTON	Five times a day; at 8 and 11 in
HOLLOWAY	the Morning, and 2, 4, and 7
	Afternoon.

From the Office for the Hermitage-Precinct, on Little Tower-hill, to

LIMEHOUSE	Three times a day; at 8 and 12
POPLAR	in the Morning, and 4 in the
BLACKWAL	Afternoon.
STEPNEY	

BOW	Twice a day; at Eight in the
STRATFORD	Morning and Two in the
UPPER and LOWER	Afternoon.
BRUMLEY	
EAST and WEST HAM	

UPTON	Once a day; at Eight in the
PLAISTOW	Morning .
GREENSTREET	

From the Office for SOUTHWARK-Precinct, in Fowl Lane
in the Borrough, to

LAMBETH-MARSH	Four times a day; at 8 and 11
LAMBETH-TOWN	in the Morning, and 2 and 6 in
SOUTH-LAMBETH	the Afternoon.
FOX-HALL	

NINE-ELMS
CLAPHAM
BATTERSEA
WANDSWORTH
PUTNEY
WIMBLETON
ROE-HAMPTON
BARNS
BARN-ELMS
MORECLACK
EAST and WEST SHEEN
RICHMOND
KEW
HAM
NEWINGTON-BUTS
KENNINGTON
WALLWORTH
CHAMBERWELL
PECKHAM
DULWICH

Twice a day; at 8 in the Morning, and Two in the Afternoon.

STOCKWELL
STRETHAM
MITCHAM
WODON
BEDDINGTON
UPPER and LOWER SHEEN
WALLINGTON
CASEHALTON
MORDEN
MARTIN
UPPER and LOWER
    TOOTING
CRAYDON

Once a day; at Eight in the Morning.

REDRIFF

Seven times a day.

| UPPER and LOWER DEPTFORD GREENWICH CHARLTON WOOLWICH PLUMSTED LEIGH LUSAM ELTHAM | Twice a day; at Eight in the Morning, and 1 in the Afternoon. |

From the General Penny-Post Office at Crosby-house in Bishopgate-street, to

| HOXDON KINGSLAND NEWINGTON-GREEN NEWINGTON-TOWN | Three times a day; at 8 and 12 in the Morning, and 5 in the Afternoon. |

| TOTTENHAM EDMONTON SOUTHGATE ENFIELD NORTHALL WALTHAM-ABBY EPPING | Once a day; at Eight in the Morning. |

| MILE-END HACKNEY ABRIDGE ONGER | Three times a day; at 8 and 12 in the Morning, and 5 in the Afternoon. |

| LOWLAYTON LAYTON-STONE WALTHAMSTOW WOODFORD CHIGWELL WANSTEAD ILLFORD BARKIN PISSINFORD-BRIDGE HARE-STREET | Once a day; at Eight in the Morning. |

And for prevention of Delays, this is further to give Notice, That such Persons as send Letters to any of the afore-mentioned Towns, and cannot conveniently deliver them into the proper Offices, are to allow a proportionable time for their conveyance from the Receiving-houses to the said Offices, from whence they are dispatcht: And such Letters that are directed to the Towns most remote, and of Consequence to be delivered in the Morning, it would be convenient they should be left over night, before the Messengers bring in their last Walks.

Note, That for every Letter and Parcel from these Towns to London, you are to pay One Penny at the Receiving-houses there: And from London to the aforesaid Towns, the Messenger is allowed for his own Pains and Care, to take a Penny for each Letter or Parcel at the delivery, and no more.

Any person (either in City or Country) that desires one of these Papers, sending to any of the above-named Six Offices, may have them delivered Gratis.

An Account of the London Penny Post

(From *The Present State of England*, 1750)

Besides the former, there is another *Post* well establish'd, call'd
the *Penny Post*, to the great Advantage of the populous City, and the
Parts adjacent. Here any Letter, or Parcel, that does not exceed
16 Ounces Weight, or the Value of ten Pounds, is not only safely,
but with the greatest Expedition, convey'd from all such Part
within the Bills of Mortality to most Towns within seven Miles
round *London*, as are not commodiously serv'd by the General Post

The Advantages arising from this, as well as of all other lawfu
Carriage of Letters belonging to his Majesty, are settled upon him
by Act of Parliament, and transacted for him by a Comptroller.

The General Office is in Threadneedle-street; and there are five
Out offices dependent upon it, commonly call'd the Sorting-Houses
that is to say, one at Westminster, one at Lincoln's Inn, a third
in an Alley near Newgate-street, the fourth near St. Mary Overs, in
Southwark; and the last, call'd the Hermitage-Office, near the
Tower.

There are about 100 Sorters and Messengers belonging to all the
Offices above mention'd; the Principal thereof is allow'd 12s per
Week; and the Sub Sorter 10s. The Town-Messengers indeed, who
collect and deliver Letters, have but 8s but those in the Country are
allow'd from 10 to 12s weekly; and there are some whose walk
being more extensive than ordinary have 15s.

There are at least 500 Shops and Coffee-houses in the City and
Country, where *Letters* and *Parcels* are taken in, and carried from
thence by the *Messengers* to their proper Office; and this is done
every two Hours: Constant Attendance is, moreover, given at al
the Offices, from Morning till Night, every Day, *Sunday* excepted.

There is one great Convenience attending these Offices, and that
is, that a Parcel of Value, in case the Office is appriz'd of the Con
176

tents, will be delive'd with all the Safety imaginable, the Office being accountable to the injur'd Party, in case it should miscarry.

And a further Convenience of this Office is, that whatsoever Letters come from all Parts of the World, by the *General Post*, directed to Persons in any of those Country-Towns to which the *Penny Post* duly goes, they are delive'd by the *Messengers* thereof the very same Day they come to *London*; and the answers if left at the *Receiving Houses*, are by them safely carried every Night to the Office in Lombard Street.

APPENDIX VII

Provincial Penny Posts

A petition was made during Queen Anne's reign asking permission for "the erecting a Penny Pacquett Office in Dublin and ten or twelve miles round it", but nothing came of it. According to an announcement in Slater's *Public Gazetteer* of January 4, 1769, "any single letter put into the Post Office will be delivered by the letter-carriers the day following, on the payment of a penny in Dublin or at any post town within ten miles thereof". This penny collection was probably a private arrangement made by the postmaster, a common enough practice in many cities.

IN DUBLIN

It was not until 1773 that a Penny Post was officially proclaimed in Dublin, the following notice appearing in *Faulkner's Dublin Journal*, Sept.–Nov., 1773:

GENERAL POST OFFICE,

DUBLIN September 28 1773

HIS Majesty's Postmaster General having been pleased to direct that, for the Benefit of the internal Correspondence of this City, a PENNY-POST shall be established therein: Notice is therefore hereby given, that, in Pursuance of such Directions, a PENNY-POST OFFICE will be established on the 11th Day of October next, subject to the following Regulations, viz:

All Letters and Packets, not exceeding the Weight of Four ounces, will be forwarded from the Penny-Post Office, in the General-Post-Office-Yard, twice every Day, Sundays excepted, viz. at nine o'clock in the Morning and four in the Afternoon, to any part of the City of Dublin, within the following Limits, viz.

Barrack-Street, to the Ferry opposite Stevens' Hospital
All Arbour-Hill and Mountpellier, to Mr. M'Mahon's house, situate on the North Side thereof, including the same.

Stonybatter, to the Turnpike in Black-horse-lane; also, to Henry Stevens Reilly's House in Prussia-street, including the same.

Glassnevin Road, to Mr. James Pettigrew's House at the Broadstone, including said House.

Drumcondra Road to the Turnpike.

Summerhill, to Sir Charles Burton's House, including the same.

Mecklenburgh-street, Gloster-street, Cumberland-street, World's-end-lane, and the Strand, to the Pound.

Sir John Rogerson's Quay to the Marine School, including the same.

Lazer's Hill to the Folly, or the Road turning to Artichoke.

Merrion-square, Hamilton's-row, Cumberland-street, and Denzill-street.

Ball's Bridge Road to Stable-lane, being Sixteen Perches from the South-end of Merrion-street, also Hume-street, and Ely Place.

Donnybrook Road or Leeson's-street, to the late Lord Cavan's House including the same.

Kevan's-port to Northumberland-street, Gordon's-lane, and Porto Bello.

New-street to the Circular Road.

Dolphin's-barn-lane, or Cork-street, to the Dipping-bridge, situate at the East-end of Dolphin's-barn-town.

All Marrowbone-lane.

James's-street, Mount Brown to the South-end of Murdering-lane.

Bow-lane, to the North-end of Murdering-lane.

A Penny is to be paid with every Letter put into the Penny-Post-Office, or into any of the Receiving-houses; for which Penny, every such Letter will be delivered to the Person to whom it is addressed, within the Limits above specified, without any further Charge; but every Letter, with which a Penny is not paid, will be opened, and returned to the Writer.

To extend as far as possible the Benefits of this Establishment, to every Part of the City, Eighteen Receiving-houses will be established at the following Places, where Letters may be put in every Day from Eight in the Morning till Ten at Night (Sundays excepted) on the Terms before-mentioned.

Mr. Daniel Kingsley, Grocer, Wormwood-gate, near New-row, Thomas-street.

Mr. Charles Wren, Hosier, at the Sign of the Stocking, Francis-street, near the Coombe.

Mr. Grogan, Grocer, Bride-street, opposite Peter-street.

Mr. Matthew Reilly, Grocer, Great Cuffe-street.

Mr. Campbell, Milliner, Anne-street, near Dawson-street.

Mr. Nowlan, Grocer, Clare-street.

Mr. Sleater, Bookseller, Castle-street.

Mr. Gallagher, Custom-house Coffee-house.

Mr. Bredberry, Grocer, at the Sign of the three Swedish Crowns, George's Quay.

Mrs. Mackerness, Grocer, at the Sign of Leicester-house, Barrack-street.

Mr. John Penton, Grocer, at the Sign of the Brave Irishman, corner of West Arran-street, near Smithfield.

Mr. James Manchester, Cheesmonger, King-street, near the Linen-hall.

Mr. Roche, Perfumer, Bolton-street, near Capel-street.

Mr. Reed, Haberdasher, Britain-street, near the Mall.

Mr. Finn, Grocer, Mary-street, near Henry-street.

Mr. Bourke, Grocer, at the Black Boy and Sugar Loaf, Capel-street, near Essex-bridge.

Mr. Gill, Shoemaker, at the Golden Boot, Abbey-street, near the Ferry.

Mr. Peter Tomlinson, Grocer, Thatched Cabbin, Big Ship-street.

Letters, containing Money or Things of Value, to be forwarded by the Penny-Post, must be delivered open to the Officer in waiting at the Penny-Post-Office, to be by him entered, otherwise the Office will not be in any Degree answerable for their Miscarriage.

All persons are requested to be as exact as possible in the Direction of Penny-Post Letters, particularly those addressed to Lodgers, and to specify the Names of the Landlord, or the Sign, which will greatly tend to facilitate their Delivery. As a further Means to answer this End, and as a Check upon the Letter-Carriers, every Letter that after a Week's Enquiry, shall be returned by them, will be opened, and sent back to the Writer, Gratis, if his or her Place of Residence can be discovered; to the End that if the Reason assigned by the Letter-Carrier, on the Cover, for the non-delivery of such Letter, does not prove satisfactory, the Writer may have an Opportunity of discovering where the Fault lay, by a Complaint to the Comptroller of the Penny-Post-Office.

By Order of the Postmaster General,

JOHN WALCOT, Secretary.

Penny-Post Office,
Comptroller, JOHN WALCOT.
First Clerk, THOMAS BOND.

The following year the area of the Penny Post was extended to places within 4 miles of the General Post Office. By the end of the century the business had declined and many of the receiving houses had closed. In 1810 the Dublin Penny Post was reorganized; its letter-carriers wore a distinctive uniform, and deliveries were made four times a day in the city, while in the country area two daily collections were made. In 1819 the limits were extended to 6 miles from the Chief Office in Sackville Street. Not being a very large city, many people used their servants for delivering local messages and letters, so that the Penny

Fig. 27. *The first penny stamps to be used in Dublin, from 1773.*

Post depended largely upon letters arriving by the General Post for delivery within the city. Dublin's Penny Post was never financially a success and was run at a loss until 1823. The 9th Report of the Commissioners on Fees and Gratuities (1810), App. 27, states that receipts averaged only £30 a week, and did not cover the expense of running it. This is probably the reason why other Penny Posts were not set up in Irish cities, for there were no others until the union of the British and Irish Post Offices in 1831. By the late 1830s there were over four hundred post towns in Ireland, of which about 140 had a Penny Post service.

Fig. 28. *Dublin Penny Post stamp of the 1830s.*

IN EDINBURGH

Edinburgh's Penny Post was due to the initiative and enterprise of Peter Williamson, who established it some time between May 1773 and May 1774. The earliest mention of this is given in the second edition of the 1774 *Edinburgh Directory*, which was published by Williamson, and was another of his enterprises.

The Publisher takes the opportunity to acquaint the Public that he will always make it his study to dispatch all letters and parcels, not exceeding three pounds in weight, to any place within an English mile to the east, south and west of the cross of Edinburgh, and as far as South and North Leith, every hour through the day, for one penny each letter or bundle.

The chief office was established near St. Giles Cathedral, at the Luckenbooths, and a number of shops within the neighbourhood

EDIN Dec. 22d. 1773.   1d.

Edinburgh's first Penny Post stamp. (Sir Walter Mercer collection.)

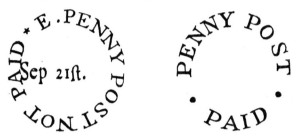

Fig. 29. *Peter Williamson's Penny Post stamps.*
Several variations of the circular stamps are known.

served as receiving houses. The Directory makes particular mention of the Penny Post stamps which Williamson introduced:

> The public will observe that the conductor of this scheme will not be answerable for any letters, or parcels, but those that are put into any of the above offices, and such as are given to his men on the streets that wear hats, with the words Penny Post on them; which letters, etc., will be marked before they are delivered, with a round stamp Penny Post Not Paid, with black ink, and those paid, with red ink, Penny Post Paid. All letters delivered by the Penny Post men without being stamped, as above, are an infringement on the master's property. If the deliverer of any letters, etc., shall presume to impose upon any person by charging more than one penny for each letter or parcel, or keeping up the letters etc., too long, such persons as are imposed upon will be so good as to give notice, and they shall have immediate redress.

The Government took over the post in 1793, when a stamp of very simple design was struck in red on Penny Post letters.

The next year other stamps were introduced which showed the times of delivery. Subsequently a number Fig. 30. of Penny Post stamps were used for Edinburgh and neighbourhood and the outlying towns of Portobello, Musselburgh, Newhaven, Preston Pans, Dalkeith, Leith, Liberton, Lasswade, etc.

In England, as a consequence of the Act of 1765, penny posts could be established in any part of the country by the Postmasters General whenever it was considered expedient. But it was not until 1793 that any advantage was taken of this provision, when in

Fig. 31. *Types of Edinburgh Penny Post stamps showing delivery times, c. 1795–1808. There were many different designs.*

February of that year plans were made to establish penny postage in Bristol, Manchester, and Birmingham, by way of experiment.

In the Minute Books preserved in the G.P.O. archives is an entry for the month of February 1793, under the heading of 'Penny Post' which says:

The principle upon which Penny Post offices in the Country Towns would be established can at first be only experimental, the primary object must be "accommodation", the second "Revenue". If the accommodation succeeds the Revenue will follow but it will be by slow degrees. As in the Infancy of such Establishments many great and unforeseen difficulties will occur. The Postmasters General's consent to make the experiment only in the three Towns pointed out by Mr. Freeling viz:—Bristol, Birmingham and Manchester. . . . The Returns made by the Surveyors must in the nature of them be insufficient, especially as the Postmasters have an interest in discouraging the P.Posts, the Postmasters therefore should be told they shall during their lives be fully compensated for the loss they may sustain of any of their emoluments in consequence of Penny Posts being established. . . .

The Manchester Deputy will have no claim for compensation being a new one and having a liberal Salary, the other two will have a fair claim to full compensation and should be made easy upon that point.

Those who call for their letters at the office must only pay 1d. if they were originally brought by the P.Post and have not passed through the General Post Office but not otherwise. . . . One great reason of its

183

answering in future in point of Revenue will be the additional correspondence it may be supposed to create for the General Post, but above all it will answer if it promotes the convenience, the interest and the Commercial intercourse of the Nation at large.

IN MANCHESTER

The first English Provincial Penny Post Office to be opened was Manchester in April 1793. An old notice preserved in the Manchester Public Library proclaims the event:

POST-OFFICE, MANCHESTER

April 8th, 1793.

HIS MAJESTY'S POST MASTER GENERAL

Having been pleased to settle and establish A PENNY POST OFFICE in the Town of Manchester, and the Suburbs thereof and Places adjacent;

Notice is hereby given, that Offices are opened for the receipt of Letters and Parcels, not exceeding four Ounces weight, at the following Places:

1st. Deansgate—near Brazen-nose Street
2nd. Salford—near Trinity Chapel
3rd. High Street near Turner Street
4th. Bank top near Piccadilly

And also at the principal Post Office in Back Square, from which Places Deliveries will be made all over the Town *Three Times a Day* viz. Eight in the Morning—Half Past Twelve at Noon—and Six in the Afternoon.—Before which Times Letters should be put into the above Offices, in order to be sent by the quickest Conveyance—for the carriage of which, one Penny will be charged in the Town, and two Pence for such as are for the Places adjacent, and within the Penny Post delivery.

Letters intended for the General Post for *London, and all Parts* may, on payment of one Penny with them, be put into any of the Four Receiving Houses, to be taken to the principal Office at the proper Times for their being circulated by the several Posts without Delay. The Receiving Houses will be open from Seven in the Morning till Ten at Night, for that Purpose; and the Postage both on Foreign and Inland paid Letters, will be received at them, the same as at the Principal Office.

Letter Carriers will be despatched regularly every Day (Sundays excepted) with the Letters to and from Middleton, Ashton-under-line, Staley-Bridge, Oldham, Saddleworth, and other Places, of which due Notice will be given.

It is the Wish of the *Post Master General* rather to prevent than to punish. Therefore that the unwary may be made acquainted with the Penalties they are subject to, by illegally conveying Letters within the Precincts of the Penny Post Delivery, the following Extract of 5th Geo. 3d. is added by their Lordships order.

"And be it further enacted by the Authority aforesaid, that when "any Penny Post Office or Offices shall be settled and established in any "Cities, Towns, Suburbs, or Places adjacent, within the Kingdoms of "*Great Britain* and *Ireland*, and the *British* Dominions in *America*, no "Person or Persons whatsoever shall make any Collection of Letters "or Packets in or near such City, Town, Suburbs, or Places, where such "Penny Office or Offices shall be established, without Licence or "Leave of the Postmaster General for the Time being; upon Pain of "incurring the Forfeitures and Penalties to be forfeited and paid by "Persons collecting, receiving, carrying, recarrying, and delivering "Letters contrary to the Act, made in the Ninth Year of the Reign of "Her late Majesty Queen *Anne*; to be recovered in Manner as by the "said Act is directed, and with Full Costs of Suit."

N.B. The Penalties to be incurred by the 9th Queen Anne, are FIVE POUNDS for every Letter, or Packet, illegally collected, carried, or delivered, *whether for Hire or not*, and ONE HUNDRED POUNDS for every Week such Practices are continued.

By Command of the Post-master General.

GEO. WESTERN,
Surveyor G.P.O.

IN BRISTOL AND BIRMINGHAM

The next to open was Bristol in July, followed by Birmingham in August. On August 27 the *London Gazette* carried this notice:

POST OFFICE BIRMINGHAM

Aug. 27 1793 H.M. Postmaster Gen: having been pleased to settle and establish a Penny Post for the convenience of this Town, the Suburbs thereof, and the Places adjacent,—NOTICE is hereby given that offices are opened for the receipt of letters and packets (not exceeding 4.Oz: in w't) from 7 in the morn'g till 9 at night in the following places

    Mr Hewitt's grocer No 48 Smallbrook St
    Mr Steven's grocer No 72 Digbeth near Deritend Bridge
    Mr Smith's grocer Church St Ludgate Hill
    Mr Murgott's grocer Coleshill St. opp Market St
    Mr Lutey's grocer Steelhouse Lane, the corner of Whittall St

From which places, Letters will be sent to the principal office opposite the Theatre in New St four times a day viz:

    At 8 in the morn'g, for the first delivery and in time to be forwarded by the North Mail via Lichfield
    At 12.0 noon for the 2nd. delivery, and in time for the mail going to Shrewsbury
    At ¼ before 2 in the afternoon, for the London Mail, and for the 3rd. delivery at ½ past 3
    At 4 in the afternoon for the Mail going to Bristol

On or before which times, letters should be put into the above Offices, in order to be sent by the earliest convenience, for which one penny will be charged in the Town, and twopence for the suburbs and places within the limit of the Penny Post, to be paid on putting in, or on delivery, at the option of the sender, except Letters intended to be forwarded by the London and Cross Road, Mails, with which, one penny must be paid on putting in to the above mentioned Receiving Houses.
    Letter Carriers will be dispatched every day (except Mon:) with the letters to and from Solihull, Knowle, Sutton C'field, Hales Owen, Dudley, West Bromwich, Tipston, Wednesbury, Darlaston, Willenhall, Bilstone and to the intermediate and adjacent places.

Numbers were allocated to the country offices within the Penny Post area up to No. 15. Of these, the following have been recorded:

    No. 1   Brierley Hill
    No. 4   Oldbury
    No. 6   Solihull
    No. 7   Knowle
    No. 8   Tipton
    No. 10   West Bromwich
    No. 11   Wednesbury
    No. 12   Sutton Coldfield
    No. 14   Castle Bromwich
    No. 15   Handsworth

Nos. 2, 3, 5, 9, and 13 have not yet been seen. Two of these were probably given to Bilston and Hales Owen, which refused to come into the scheme. The inhabitants of both these places opposed the plan because under their existing local arrangements they were already served by a cheap local delivery, sometimes paying only a halfpenny for a local letter.

Manchester	*Bristol*	*Birmingham*
No. 6 believed to be Saddle-worth (1794).	*A similar stamp shows P.P.U. denoting Penny Post Unpaid (1805).*	*No. 12 Sutton Coldfield (1793).*

Fig. 32. *The first English Provincial Penny Post stamps.*

With the opening of Penny Post Offices at Manchester, Bristol, and Birmingham, each of these places introduced a special hand-stamp for marking penny post letters. These early stamps are very uncommon and difficult to find on letters of the late eighteenth century. Other cities were also considered for a penny post service, but, following reports made by the Post Office surveyors were not recommended. Bath, Norwich, Exeter, and Liverpool were all turned down, the last named "owing to its peculiar situation". Not until the turn of the century were other Penny Post Offices established in other cities. By the 1820s the rush was on, with penny posts opening up everywhere, so that by the 1830s nearly every post town in the kingdom had its own penny post. Villages, too, were given their own named penny post stamps, though the custom of using a numbered stamp, as for example, "No 7", for a receiving house or a sub-office was very common. Sometimes merely the name stamp of a place was used, such as OLD DOWN, between Bath and Bristol.

Letters would be brought to the post-town head office to be stamped with its penny post stamp, and then sent on. Some Penny Post cities covered a very wide area, such as Bristol, which was served by nearly 60 sub-offices. Exeter had 43, Manchester 37, and Glasgow nearly 30.

Although the use of penny post stamps became unnecessary after 1840, they continued in use right up to 1856 in some places.

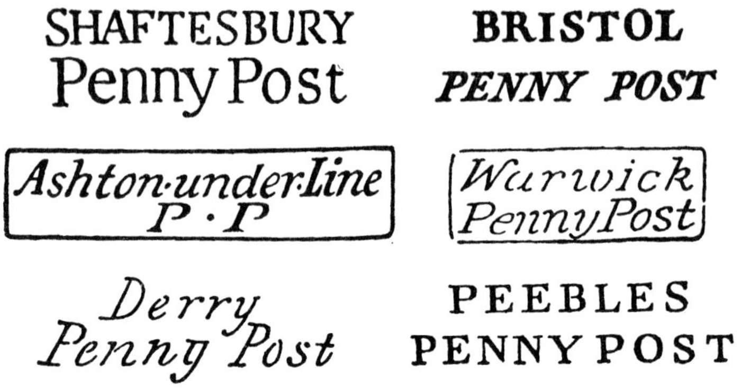

SHAFTESBURY
Penny Post

BRISTOL
PENNY POST

Ashton-under-Line
P · P

Warwick
PennyPost

Derry
Penny Post

PEEBLES
PENNY POST

Fig. 33. *A selection of Penny Post stamps showing types in use from about 1812 to the 1830s. Red or black ink was generally used, though green and blue were used in some places.*

APPENDIX VIII

Uniform Penny Postage Stamps

When uniform penny postage came into force on January 10, 1840, the proposed adhesive stamps for franking letters were not ready. Many post offices throughout the kingdom improvised by using hand-stamps of varying design, denoting the One Penny Paid (in a few cases—2d.), and some offices used "Paid" and "Penny Post" stamps (as a rule applied in red ink) which had been in common use for some years. But at many post offices letters were handed in over the counter and the post office clerk wrote on in red ink—"Pd 1d"—sometimes merely scrawling a downstroke 1.

Under the new regulations all letters had to be pre-paid, so the public began a new custom by marking their envelopes in one of the corners—"Prepaid" or, simply "P.P.". A few enterprising stationers issued envelopes specially printed (see Plate 12a), and sometimes ornamental in design bearing the words "PRE-PAID" or with the PRE-PAID showing against a decorated embossed background, usually delicately designed. Such items have become real collectors' pieces, and are eagerly looked for.

Whereas the "Penny Paid" hand-stamps are well known and have mostly been recorded (though new specimens are still to be found), another set of hand-stamps is not so generally known (see Fig. 34). These stamps are extremely simple in design and are usually very small in size. Very few have been recorded, and they seem to have made their appearance on or about January 10. The rarest are worded PREPAID, the more general ones simply "Paid" in small serifed letters sometimes within a frame.

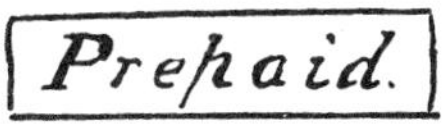

Prepaid.	Paid.	PAID
St. James St. P.O., London (in red).	Alresford (in black).	West Bromwich (in red).

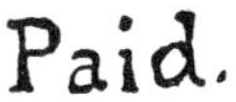

Fig. 34. *Uniform Penny Post stamps.*

These little Pre-paid and Paid stamps did not remain in use for long, for there was really no need for them once the adhesive stamps were in general use. However, a few towns, notably Norwich and Portsmouth, continued to use them until the late 1840s.

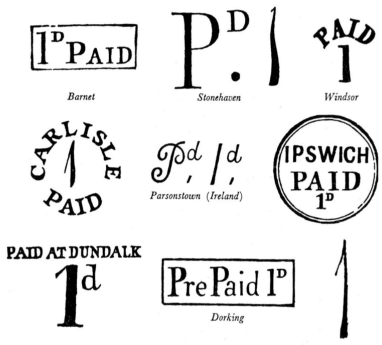

Fig. 35. *A selection of uniform Penny Postage stamps. Almost every town and city in the Kingdom had its own design. Some stamps remained in use until 1853, when adhesive stamps were made compulsory. Red or black ink was commonly used.*

Elihu Burritt's Campaign for an Ocean Penny Postage

Elihu Burritt published several pamphlets during his campaign and advocated an ocean rate of one penny for carrying a letter from any port in the United Kingdom to any port overseas used by the British mail packets, and vice versa.

> It would meet the terms of our proposition if every letter under half an ounce, from any town in Gt. Britain to any town in the Colonies, should pay *three-pence*; one penny for the home inland rate, another penny for the ocean, and the third for the colonial inland rate, and *vice versa*. The Government now charges one shilling for these rates.

Pictorial envelopes and note-paper advocating Ocean Penny Postage were widely used throughout the campaign, and proved very effective propaganda. They were published by well-known firms, all sympathetic to the cause—Charles Gilpin in London, Bradshaw & Blacklock of Manchester, famous for railway time-tables, and Valentines of Dundee, a firm which later became well known for picture postcards. It is mainly because of these pictorial envelopes that Elihu Burritt's work and endeavours have been remembered. People saved them and put them away in desks and drawers; later, when the collecting of Mulready envelopes and their caricatures became popular, these Ocean Penny Postage envelopes were also sought after. The first comprehensive list and description about them appeared in a book *The Mulready Envelope and its Caricatures*, by Major Edward Evans, published in 1891. In 1897 M. Moens, a Brussels stamp dealer and publisher, listed them in his catalogue. He also reprinted them, making excellent imitations. Although slight differences can be observed in the designs, they are easily discernible from the originals, as the name "F. Deracdc-maeker" is always shown in very small lettering somewhere along the lower part of the designs. Since that time these propaganda envelopes have become favourites with collectors in all parts of the world, and their value increases every year. At the time of writing the market value of an ordinary specimen, postally used and in clean condition, is about £12 to £20, but £30 to £50 is not unusual for one of the rarer kinds. The Moens reproductions are worth only a few shillings.

Plate 20a. Published by Bradshaw & Blacklock of Manchester.

Five types of this design are known. They vary slightly one from the other, by reason of the publisher's printed name and description, slight variations in the text, the colour of the paper (azure, white and buff), and difference in size. It was a popular design, which accounts for more having survived of this series than many of the others.

Plate 20b. Published by Charles Gilpin, 5 Bishopsgate Street Without, London.

This envelope was drawn by the artist Henry Anelay, and is one which is more frequently seen. There are two varieties, with a different publisher's inscription.

Plate 21a. Also published by Charles Gilpin. A smaller variety of Plate 20b and less common.

Plate 21b. Published by J. Valentine of Dundee.

More pictorial envelopes were produced by this firm than by any other, and numerous printings were made of all the designs, so that a great many differences exist. The major variation of the one shown in the illustration is the omission of the shipping, which, in the original, extends across the lower part of the envelope. This design is the commonest of all the Ocean Penny Postage envelopes.

Plate 22a. Published by J. Valentine of Dundee.

An envelope with an overall design printed on the back, on greyish paper leaving the address side quite clear. No variations so far recorded. This example is very uncommon, and scarce in used condition.

Plate 22b. Published by E. Myers & Co.

Three varieties exist of this envelope. One has the imprint "Myers & Compy., London" in the bottom left-hand corner;

Plate 20*a*. Published by Bradshaw & Blacklock of Manchester.

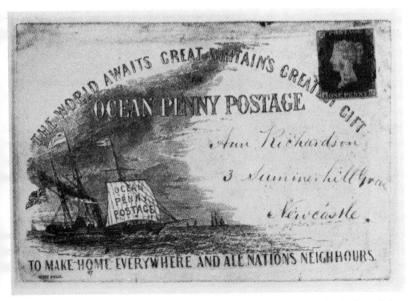

Plate 20*b*. Published by Charles Gilpin of London, and designed by
Henry Anelay, a prominent member of Elihu Burritt's movement.

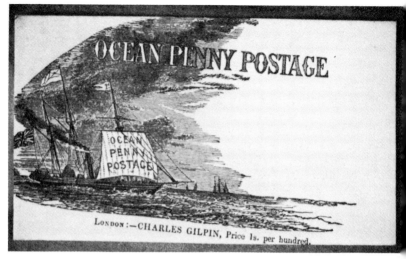

Plate 21a. One of the less-known designs.

Plate 21b. Published by J. Valentine of Dundee. A variation of this shows the shipping extended to the right-hand corner.

another has "Ackerman & Co., Johnston & Hunter. J. Valentine" on the back, while the third has, in addition, "Hudson Scott and R. Theobald". All are printed on greyish-white paper, and are uncommon.

Plate 23a. Published by the League of Universal Brotherhood.

This is another of the scarce Ocean Penny Postage envelopes. It carries the imprint of "Mitchell, Lovells Ct. Paternoster Row" in the lower front corner. Another, exactly similar in design, has this inscription also on the flap, and a third variety has "London: Office of League of Brotherhood, 3 Winchester Buildings, City. 7d per packet of 25." The flaps of all three types are embossed with a small oval seal showing a pair of clasped hands surrounded by LEAGUE OF UNIVERSAL BROTHERHOOD. Copies are known of the seal printed in pink, blue, and brown, and uncoloured. A second design of this type is known, having a much shorter banner. It is extremely rare.

Plate 23b. Published by The New York Cheap Postage Association.

This example is the only one known to have been published in the United States. Embellished with the American eagle, and showing a train along the upper half of the envelope, with a mail steamer in the bottom left-hand corner, it is inscribed along the top: "We ask of Congress Cheap Inland and Ocean Postage". It is one of the rarest of all the propaganda envelopes.

The pictorial writing-paper used with some of the envelopes is not often seen, and not easy to come by. Two designs only are known. One is headed with the picture of a mail steamer, similar to the Bradshaw and Blacklock design; the other shows a mail steamer bearing down in a tempestuous sea, and bears the inscription: "Fair speed the Ship whose signal is unfurled. An 'OCEAN PENNY POSTAGE' for the world."

All these propaganda envelopes were used from 1849 onwards, into the 1860s. Sometimes they were used many years afterwards, but the campaign was at its height during the 1850s. Burritt's first pamphlet on Ocean Penny Postage was published in 1846, and from then on he published several. He operated from offices in No. 27 New Broad Street, London (according to a letter in the author's ownership), and organized the Peace Campaign from No. 19 New

Broad Street. Later, evidence suggests that his offices were in No. 35 Broad Street Buildings. Public meetings in support of Ocean Penny Postage were held in the major cities of the United Kingdom; according to a statement in one of his pamphlets, nearly 150 took place, usually presided over by the mayor, assisted by influential people of all callings.

Although nothing came of the idea, the agitation which it caused was responsible for the memory of it lingering in people's minds for a good many years. Undoubtedly the campaign paved the way for that other project, Imperial Penny Postage, which was ultimately achieved in 1898.

APPENDIX X

Claimants to Sir Rowland Hill's Fame

In the *Dictionary of National Biography* it is stated that the Rev. Samuel Roberts, the Welsh social and political reformer, memorialized the Post Office from 1827 onwards for a system of inland penny postage, together with a proportional reduction (3*d.* per ounce) for an ocean postage, and that Roberts corresponded with Elihu Burritt on the subject. In a book written by Roberts he says that "it is a fact that the atmosphere in and around the G.P.O. and around many other high places in London was full of Samuel Roberts schemes of Penny Postage, more than ten years before Sir Rowland Hill had appeared in the field". Commenting on Ocean Penny Postage, Roberts claims to have been interested in proportionate reduction of Ocean Penny Postage fifteen years before Elihu Burritt began his campaign from London.

Glanmer Williams, in a biography entitled *Samuel Roberts of Llanbrynmair*,[1] cautiously handles these statements by saying "we cannot be sure whether it was Samuel Roberts or Sir Rowland Hill (who usually gets the credit) or someone else who was the first to think of the scheme. Samuel Roberts always claimed that he had suggested it in print some years before Sir Rowland."

In 1883, thanks to the efforts of friends and admirers "to cheer him in his old age and affliction", Roberts received a testimonial of £400 in recognition of all he had done for postal reform. Among the list of subscribers was the name of Mr. Gladstone, who gave £50. Roberts always believed that this represented government recognition of his efforts!

A more remarkable claim was that of Francis Worrell Stevens. On July 17, 1889, a petition was presented to the House of Commons by the Marquis of Carmarthen, the Member of Parliament for Brixton, "on behalf of Mr. Francis Worrell Stevens, the real Inventor

[1] University of Wales Press, Cardiff, 1950.

of the Penny Postage System". Stevens requested that a search should be made among the records of the Chancellor of the Exchequer's Office, and his service as originator of the Penny Postage stamp plan be acknowledged. This lengthy document states that Stevens wrote to Lord Althorpe, the Chancellor of the Exchequer, at Downing Street, in 1833, suggesting how postage could be collected by means of stamps sold in advance, and submitted a design for a postage stamp with the likeness of King William IV on it. It was explained that at that time Rowland Hill was an assistant master at his school, Albion House, Loughton, in Essex, and that Stevens had discussed his plan and shown the correspondence to Hill. Hill requested Stevens to lend him the papers to read through, saying "it was a capital subject for a pamphlet", and asked his permission to write one based on his (Stevens) plan. Stevens lent Rowland Hill his papers, school broke up for the holidays, and they parted.

The petition goes on to explain how Stevens again met Hill, who told him he was waiting for the Government to send for him; he had finished writing the pamphlet, which only required Stevens corrections and signature to it. After this Stevens says he never saw Hill again. Stevens emigrated to New Zealand, and gave little thought to the matter, until many years later, in 1876, he was informed of the honours and reward which had been bestowed on Rowland Hill.

Thereupon he wrote to Rowland Hill demanding how he dared assert to be the inventor and originator of Penny Postage when he knew to the contrary. Hill never replied to this letter.

Stevens referred to Hill as an impostor, saying that the country had been cheated and swindled and requested that all the statues erected in his honour should be pulled down. The petition concluded with the petitioner praying that something might yet be done for him.

In the light of what is factually known about Rowland Hill and his postal reform and the many people concerned with him, it is extraordinary that the Marquis of Carmarthen should have championed the cause of this man.

Written on the back of this printed petition, which is contained among papers in the G.P.O. records room, is "P.M.G. does not propose to take any action in the matter".

The claims of Francis Worrell Stevens were again made public in a curious booklet entitled *A Corner of Epping Forest, and the Origin of the Penny Post*, by H. V. Wiles, published about 1948 by the West Essex Printing Co. Ltd.

The claim made by Patrick Chalmers on behalf of his father James Chalmers as inventor of the postage stamp has been the subject of considerable controversy. James Chalmers was a bookseller in Dundee, who had for long been interested in postal matters. In 1837 he submitted plans for a uniform rate of postage to Mr. Wallace, the M.P. for Greenock, who had raised the question of postal reform in the House of Commons. On December 9, 1837, Mr. Wallace wrote to him acknowledging the receipt "of stamps to carry into effect Mr. Hill's plan of Postage reduction", and added "these and several others I have received will be duly submitted to the Committee on Postage".[1] Chalmers recommended the use of adhesives in the form of squared pieces of paper, printed in strips to be cut as required. In 1839 he submitted others of a circular design, for the Treasury competition. He has been referred to as "The father of the postage stamp".

After Rowland Hill's death in 1879 a long controversy took place between Pearson Hill, the son of Sir Rowland Hill, and Patrick Chalmers, the son of James Chalmers, as to who invented Penny Postage and the adhesive stamp. Numerous pamphlets and letters were published, and the argument was kept going for many years.

[1] A facsimile of this letter was published by Patrick Chalmers in support of his father's claim.

The Jubilee of Inland Uniform Penny Postage

The year 1890 was the fiftieth year of Uniform Penny Postage, and was celebrated in a grand manner in London, with two splendid functions taking place, as well as several dinners and parties for the enjoyment of those in Post Office circles. Throughout the kingdom the Jubilee was celebrated by hundreds of provincial Post Offices, the festivities more or less conforming to a general pattern. In nearly every case the celebration began with the singing of the National Anthem, followed by an address, and then a concert or fireworks, with a supper or refreshments afterwards for the staff.

The descriptions of these celebrations, which were all recorded and officially reported to Headquarters, reveal that some places were more enterprising than others. In Bedale there were "Cheers at the Market Cross", and in Berwick, a meeting of the public outside the Post Office. Some Post Offices held a dance or a social gathering, but at Walmer Road Office in Deal a gratuity was given to every postman. In Farnworth a salute was fired, and those of the staff of the Bradford Office who were returning at 10 p.m. from special duty contributed to the occason by giving cheers in the train; we are not told whether they had previously celebrated.

The first important event in the Jubilee year was purely an official one, when a dinner was held at the Holborn Restaurant in London, on January 15. This was attended by the Postmaster General, the Rt. Hon. H. C. Raikes, M.P., and many important Post Office notabilities, as well as some 250 past and present Post Office officials. Many laudatory speeches were made about the good work carried out by the Post Office, and much praise was given to the achievement of Sir Rowland Hill. It was at this dinner that the Postmaster General, in making his speech, referred to the question of Imperial Penny Postage, declaring it to be quite impracticable.

During the early part of the summer the Corporation of the City of London sent out several thousand invitations to a widely representative selection of the public to attend a Conversazione at Guildhall, on May 16, 17, and 19. The first day was a special one, honoured by the presence of the Prince of Wales.

A great deal of trouble went into making this a most agreeable event. Between intervals of orchestral music and the singing of the Post Office Choir, people were able to see a representation of a Post Office of 1790 and to compare it with a fully equipped one of 1890, complete with its telegraphic apparatus. The old Post Office of 1790 was furnished with many original antique pieces, and had genuine old postal notices and instructions on the walls. A most excellent exhibition of postal history was provided which included models of mail-coaches, mail-steamers, and Packet-boats; a travelling Post Office, old postal notices, stamps, pictures, prints and books, and all manner of curious and interesting things connected with the Post Office. It was the first exhibition of Postal History ever to be shown. During the three days of the Conversazione (which was an evening affair) some 21,000 people visited Guildhall, most of them by invitation. The enthusiasm shown for the exhibition was tremendous, and one of the highlights was a special postcard which was issued. This was printed in red, appropriately inscribed for the event, and showed the coat of arms of the City of London. A penny stamp was printed in the right-hand corner. Only 10,000 of these cards were issued and were quickly sold at sixpence each, for the benefit of the Rowland Hill Memorial Benevolent Fund. These cards are interesting, for they represent the first attempt made by our Post Office to commemorate an event, and are the forerunners of all our special commemorative postage stamps, which are now issued fairly regularly. A specially designed date-stamp was used for cancelling them, which proved to be very popular. An official report of the occasion describes how eager the public were to get examples of these special postmarks. When the 10,000 commemorative postcards were sold out 20,500 ordinary postcards were sold, the public presenting them to the Exhibition Post Office counter to have them stamped with the Guildhall cancellation. Not only postcards but anything which would take an impression was presented—programmes, pieces of paper, telegraph forms, and visiting cards, a charge of one penny being made, the proceeds going to the Benevolent Fund. So keen was the desire for these souvenir postmarks that all sorts of postage stamps were used, regardless of value. One person used stamps up to the £5 value, and a few offered the old penny black stamps.

Letters which had already been through the post in 1840 were once again posted, with the addition of the current postage stamp,

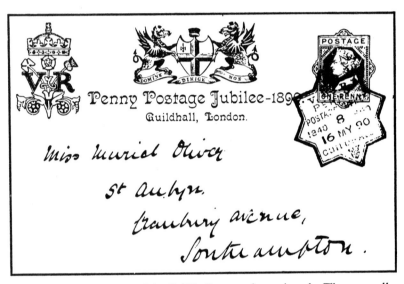

Fig. 36. *Only 10,000 of the Guildhall postcard were issued. They were all sold within an hour!*

and went back to the same address, showing the two date-stamps of 1840 and 1890. In the special report written about the Conversazione by Mr. R. C. Tombs, an eminent Post Office official and historian, one young gentleman is described handing up in his haste a small sheet of paper, pulled from out of his pocket to be date-stamped, but was somewhat abashed when he saw it was an unpaid tailor's bill. A young lady offered her pocket handkerchief, asking for it to be stamped in the corner. One unfortunate person wrote a reply post-card to the Guildhall Post Office with a message—"Have come many miles, cannot get in, please post reply half of card and oblige—DISAPPOINTED".

Considering that stamp collecting at that time—let alone the study of postal history—was not indulged in as seriously as it is today, the interest shown by the public in this sort of souvenir is quite remarkable; for all accounts of the exhibition describe the special Post Office there as being besieged and crowded the whole time. It was rumoured that these special postmarks and the postcard would one day become scarce and worth a lot of money, which quite likely explained the frenzy to get them.

Altogether some 25,000 people visited the exhibition. On the opening day the function was held in the evening, but on the other two days the public visited it during the morning and afternoon as well.

An artist's drawing in the *Illustrated London News* recording the event shows a group of visitors in evening dress looking at the lady telegraphists at work, and helps one to visualize the agreeable spectacle the whole scene must have presented, taking place as it did in historic Guildhall.

Newspapers have left us with graphic accounts of the Guildhall Conversazione, all written more or less in the same vein, an exception being that from *Punch* (May 31, 1890):

> Everybody, from the Prince of Wales hisself, down to the werry 'umblest postman or sorter, left that nobel old Hall, estonished, and dilited, and 'appy.
>
> And no wunder, for, by the combined efforts of the hole Copperashun and its werry numerus staff, and the hole army of postmen, and tellacram men, and all manner of sorters and stampers, St. Martin's-le-Grand was removed boddily to Gildall, and everything that was ever done in the one place was dun in the other before the estonished eyes of sum two thousand of us, even includin' four-horse male coaches, with sacks of letters, and reel gards with reel horns, which they blowed most butifully. It was a gloreous Jewbelee! I'm that bizzy I hardly noes wich way to turn first, so no more at pressant, from yores trewly,
>
> ROBERT

The last great Jubilee event was held on July 2 at the South Kensington Museum (Imperial Institute), when a Conversazione took place in the evening. Elaborate preparations were made for the arrival of the Duke and Duchess of Edinburgh, who were the guests of honour among a thoroughly representative selection of the public. From all accounts, the building was a beautiful sight to see, sparkling with electric lights and the galleries "crowded with a numerous and genteel company". Royal Mail vans, horsed and with lamps alight, were stationed at various points between the Museum and the Cromwell Road, and there was a Guard of Honour of the 24th Middlesex (Post Office) Rifle Volunteers, with their Regimental band.

This time, fewer postal exhibits were shown, but there were many more Post Office counters opened in different parts of the building, where a considerable business was done. Once again, an old-time Post Office of 1790 was exhibited, but a novelty was the Post Office of the future, of 1990, where several amusing and interesting glimpses into the future were shown, forecasting the speed and efficiency of the Post Office of a hundred years hence. Orchestral music and the Post Office Choir entertained the assembly throughout the course of the evening.

With the success and popularity of the Guildhall postcard in mind, the authorities had prepared for this occasion a special one-penny-stamped envelope with a correspondence card inside. This was sold for one shilling. Some 250,000 were issued and were on sale, not only at the South Kensington Museum during the course of the evening but at the London Post Offices as well throughout the day. Altogether, about 150,000 were sold, the proceeds going as before to the Rowland Hill Benevolent Fund. Like the Guildhall card, they were very popular, but the public showed greater interest in the commemorative date-stamp used to cancel them. There was a very great demand for this, and separate impressions, which were applied to programmes, cards, and anything that would take them, were charged at one penny each. Indeed, the authorities this time were well aware of the popularity of special postmarks, for no fewer than five different ones, ornamental in design, were used, including two for a "Tube Post", which was another of the novelties.

Some of the correspondence cards were sent through the post, with halfpenny postage stamps affixed, or with no stamps on at all, rendering them liable to surcharge, for many people believed them to be postcards. At this time it was not permitted to send any card through the post other than the official stamped halfpenny postcards, and these correspondence cards were, in a sense, pictorial with a

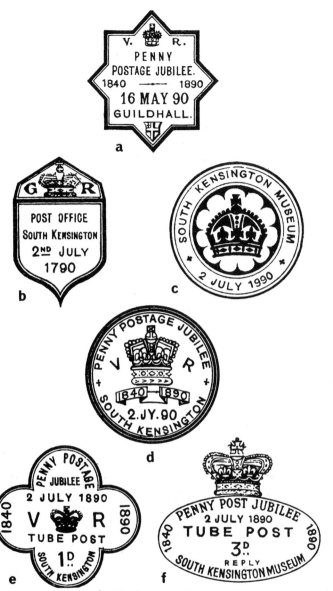

Fig. 37. *Jubilee souvenir postmarks.*

a. *The Guildhall cancellation.*

b. *Souvenir postmark of the Post Office of 1790.*

c. *Souvenir postmark of the Post Office of the future—1990 (both these markings were applied in blue ink).*

d. *The cancellation used at South Kensington Museum.*

e and f. *Souvenir postmarks of the "Electrotubular-lightning Express", used in conjunction with the Post Office of 1990.*

printed message on them, and therefore quite out of order for use as postcards.

The Jubilee envelope and card were printed in blue by Thos. De La Rue & Co. The envelope showed a pictorial comparison of the postal service of 1840 with that of 1890, and the card, with the Royal Arms in the centre, carried a picture of Sir Rowland Hill in the top left-hand corner, inscribed "He gave us Penny Postage" (see Plate 19a).

Two imitations of this envelope and card were printed privately. The first, published by a Mr. Elliott, was a fairly close copy of the original, though its pictorial features were somewhat different. In the space intended for the postage stamp was printed a small pictorial design with the legend, over and above it, "Postage One Penny". This inscription rendered it illegal, and it was promptly suppressed. The other imitation was designed by the well-known artist, Harry Furniss, and the envelope and card are very clever burlesques of the original (see Plate 19b). Although humorous, they serve to remind us that all was not harmony and well-being in the Post Office during Jubilee year, for they reveal that the postmen were underpaid and overworked. There were several disturbances to mar the celebrations, with threats of the postmen striking for better pay and conditions. On July 10 about a hundred postmen at the parcel-post depot at Clerkenwell were dismissed for attacking and expelling about seventy non-union men. Altogether some 130 men were dismissed in other districts for insubordination. Later in the year about 240 clerks in the Savings Bank department were suspended for refusing to work overtime.

These Jubilee envelopes and cards, as well as the imitations, are quite common, although the latter (especially the Elliott envelope) are scarce in postally used condition, with, of course one-penny stamps affixed to them, to carry them through the post.

Many people today, looking at these Harry Furniss caricatures are amused by the drawings, but are quite unaware of their significance.

Altogether, some 4,000 people of all walks in life attended the South Kensington Museum for the Penny Postage Jubilee. We are told that there were several postmen there with their wives and families who had come from distant places, such as Cornwall,

THE POSTAL JUBILEE.

TO THE PUBLIC.

YOU are asked to visit South Kensington Museum to celebrate the Jubilee of the Uniform Penny Post. Before doing so, consider the following facts:—

The Post Office employs men five or six hours a day for 9s. to 13s. a week, and these hours are so spread over the whole day that few of them can get other employment.

It pays many men 16s. for a week's hard work.

It pays all the Parcel Postmen in London (over 500) 18s. a week, except a few, who get 19s.

A Postman's wage is 18s. a week at starting.

Over half the Postmen in London are paid less than the rate for unskilled labour established by the Dock Workers.

None of them get a decent wage until they have been twelve or fifteen years in the service, and hundreds of them will continue, according to the present arrangement, at 16s. or 18s. all their lives. In the country they are even worse off.

The day's work is so badly arranged that it stretches over fourteen to sixteen hours.

For holding public meetings under the auspices of their Union, to make their grievances known, Postmen are being persecuted by Mr. Raikes in a most cruel and tyrannical manner.

You are asked to congratulate yourselves and the Statesmen whom you will meet there on the fact that, by overworking the Postal Employés, by defrauding them of the just reward of their labour, and stifling their complaints, you are able—not content with the Penny Post—to wring over three millions a year profit for the national exchequer. The profits of the Conversazione are for a charitable purpose, but you will be very great hypocrites indeed if you let that comfort you. Charity in itself is the most excellent of all kinds of virtue, but as a substitute for justice it is the most hateful of all kinds of humbug. The Postmen would not need your charity if they got the due price of their labour.

Think of these facts, and as many of you as can find delight in grinding the faces and gagging the voices of the poor, go to the Jubilee Conversazione.

Issued by the Postmen's Union, 58 Chancery Lane, W.C., July 1, 1890.

Fig. 38. *A little-known hand bill that appeared at the time of the Postal Jubilee. Written on the back of the one in the G.P.O. archives is:* "This circular was distributed broadcast outside South Kensington Museum last evening—the Volunteers and Police seemed to enjoy the fuss. D.W.S." *(Courtesy: H.M. Postmaster General.)*

Morpeth, and Durham, and the sight of mothers with babies in arms was commented on. It seems the fond parents hoped that their children would one day attend the Centenary of Penny Postage, and would be able to say they were present at the Jubilee.

APPENDIX XII

The Centenary of Uniform Penny Postage

The Post Office planned a celebration for the centenary of Uniform Penny Postage in 1940, but the outbreak of the Second World War made this impossible. However, the event was not allowed to pass unnoticed. On January 10 the Postal History Society commemorated the centenary by holding a dinner at Oddenino's Hotel in London. Due to the existing war-time regulations, not more than one hundred guests were allowed to assemble; among these was Colonel Henry W. Hill, C.M.G., D.S.O., who acknowledged the toast to his grandfather, Sir Rowland Hill. "The Memory of James Chalmers"—to whom some credit is given for having suggested adhesive labels for postage stamps—was proposed in a toast, and the response was made by his granddaughter, Miss Leah Chalmers. During the course of the evening a telegram was received with the message: "Best wishes for successful evening from F. Burton Osborn only surviving steward of the 50th anniversary of penny postage at Imperial Institute", thereby linking the glittering Jubilee of 1890 with the restricted celebration of 1940.

Largely due to the publicity given to this occasion, the national Press recorded January 10 with suitable phrases praising Sir Rowland Hill and the campaign for Uniform Penny Postage, otherwise the more serious news of those days might have caused the event to pass unnoticed. It was largely due to the effort of the Postal History Society that the Post Office did not abandon the idea of a special issue of a set of six stamps—½d. to 3d., which showed a design with the heads of Queen Victoria and King George VI. These were issued on May 6 precisely one hundred years since the famous one-penny black stamp was used for Uniform Penny Postage. A few days previously the inland rate of 1½d. was increased to 2½d., a fact which was commented on as being most inopportune during centenary celebrations. But, to use an oft-repeated phrase of those days, "there was a war on".

As part of the centenary celebrations a loan exhibition organized by the Royal Philatelic Society was on view at Lancaster House in London. The theme of the exhibition was the birth and evolution of the adhesive postage stamp. Exhibits came from the King's collection, the muniment room of the General Post Office, and the Henry Cole Bequest in the Victoria and Albert Museum, and from some members of the Royal Philatelic Society. It was opened by H.R.H. the Duchess of Gloucester on May 6 and lasted one week. Another Exhibition took place in Bournemouth on the same date under the auspices of the Postal History Society, and a splendid display of postal history was given. This was opened by Sir Rowland Hill's grandson, Colonel Henry W. Hill.

At both these exhibitions souvenir envelopes were on sale, special postmarks being provided for cancelling them at the exhibition Post Offices. Souvenirs in the way of miniature sheets of specially designed labels, resembling postage stamps, were also available, and at Bournemouth excellently engraved reproductions of the famous penny black and twopenny blue stamps were on sale. The proceeds from both these exhibitions were given to the funds of the British Red Cross and the Order of St. John.

Abroad, despite the universal upset caused by the war, a few countries, notably Portugal, Cuba, and Paraguay, issued postage stamps with the portrait of Sir Rowland Hill to commemorate the world's first postage stamp. Other countries brought out specially designed envelopes and postcards and used a suitably worded postmark in honour of the occasion. Even Denmark, although invaded by Germany in April 1940, was able to remember the centenary and, thanks to one of the leading Danish newspapers and the Copenhagen Philatelic Club, an exhibition was arranged and a special postcard was issued showing a large penny black postage stamp. Germany, too, produced a special postcard in honour of the occasion, but gave no mention of Rowland Hill; instead the portrait of Heinrich von Stephan, Germany's own postal reformer, was shown, in connection with postcards which had originated in Austria!

It is very probable, however, that had it not been for the efforts made by a few interested people, the centenary of Penny Postage in Great Britain might have received scarcely any official recognition and would have passed by with little mention.

Plate 22a. A scarce design printed on the back of the envelope, combining Ocean Penny Postage, Universal Brotherhood, and Peace. Designed and engraved by J. Valentine of Dundee.

Plate 22b. Published by E. Myers & Company, London.

Plate 23a. Published by the League of Universal Brotherhood.

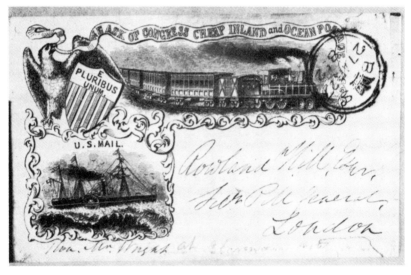

Plate 23b. The Barnabas Bates envelope, published by The New York Cheap Postage Association. One of the rarest of the propaganda envelopes. (*In the collection of Gerald Wellburn, Duncan, B.C.*)

A Table of Useful Dates

1635 Inland posts first established and postage rates fixed. Thomas Witherings "General Post Master".

1654 The franking privilege begins.

1657 The Post Office established by Act of Parliament.

1659 First suggestion of a Penny Post proposed by John Hill in a pamphlet.

1660 The Post Office Act (12 Car 11, cap. 35) frequently referred to as the Post Office charter.

1661 The first date-stamp introduced by Henry Bishop, Postmaster General.

1680 Wm. Dockwra and Robert Murray set up a Penny Post in London, March 27, and introduce the first paid hand-stamp for franking letters.

1682 December. The Government takes over the Penny Post.

1709 Charles Povey sets up a "Half-Penny Carriage" for letters. Bellmen used for letter collection in the London streets.

1711 The London Penny Post established by Act of Parliament, and limited to within 10 miles of the G.P.O.

1716 Death of William Dockwra.

1720 April—Ralph Allen takes control of the cross posts for England and Wales.

1730 A second penny on delivery of a letter by the Penny Post made legal (4 Geo. 11, cap. 33).

1764 Newspapers carried free when franked by a Member of Parliament.

1765 Penny Posts allowed to be set up anywhere in the G.P.O. administration. A penny rate for the first stage, about 15 miles.

1773 Peter Williamson sets up a Penny Post in Edinburgh. A Penny Post starts in Dublin.

1784 August 2—The first mail-coach runs from Bristol to London.

1792 The G.P.O. in London put letter carriers into uniform.

1793 Penny Posts started in Manchester, Bristol, and Birmingham. The Government takes over Peter Williamson's Edinburgh Penny Post.

1794 Re-organization of the London Penny Post by Edward Johnson.

1795 A Penny Post for soldiers and seamen. (Act of 35 Geo. III, cap. 53.)

1801 The London Penny Post becomes the Twopenny Post.

1830 Letters carried for the first time by train, between Manchester and Liverpool.

1833 Robert Wallace, M.P., attacks the Post Office in Parliament, advocates reforms.

1836 A pre-paid letter sheet used for local delivery in Philadelphia, U.S.A.

1837 Rowland Hill's pamphlet published on postal reform.

1837 The use of adhesive stamps for pre-payment of letters suggested by Rowland Hill, also by James Chalmers of Dundee.

1839 The Treasury Competition for suitable designs of stamps and covers for pre-payment of letters.

1839 December 5 to January 9, 1840—An experimental fourpenny post. In London the Twopenny Post again becomes a Penny Post.

1840 January 10—Uniform Penny Postage proclaimed. The franking privilege abolished.
May 6—The first adhesive penny stamp used on letters.

1842 United States first adhesive stamp issued by the New York City Despatch Post.

1843 First Christmas card in England, devised by Henry Cole.

1845 July 1—Postage rates reduced in the United States.

1846 Last year of the bell postmen in the London streets.

1847 United States Post Office Department issues adhesive postage stamps.

1847 Ocean Penny Postage campaign begun by Elihu Burritt.

1853 Colonial Penny Postage Association formed.

1854 Rowland Hill becomes Secretary of the Post Office. In

March G.P.O. reduces postage rates to several British Colonies.

1860   Rowland Hill knighted for his services to the nation.

1864   Sir Rowland Hill retires from the Post Office.

1870   October 1—Halfpenny postcards introduced in Great Britain.

1872*   Inland rate: 1*d.* for the first ounce.

1875   Universal Postal Union established; a $2\frac{1}{2}d.$ rate settled for foreign letters.

1879   Death of Sir Rowland Hill.

1883   October 1—The equivalent of uniform penny postage established throughout the U.S.A.

1886   Henniker Heaton, M.P., champions a Universal Penny Postage system.

1897*   Inland rate: 1*d.* up to 4 ounces.

1898   December 25—Imperial Penny Postage proclaimed to most places in the Empire.

1899   September 1—Cape Colony joins the Imperial Penny Postage system.

1901   January 1—New Zealand joins the Imperial Penny Postage system.

      June 1—Penny Postage in British ships at sea.

1905   April 1—A Penny Post from the United Kingdom to Australia, one way only.

1908   October 1—A Penny Post to and from the United Kingdom and the United States.

1911   May 1—Australia joins the Imperial Penny Postage system.

1915*   November 1—Inland rate: 1*d.* for the first ounce.

1918   June 2—The last day of uniform penny postage.

  *   June 3—Inland rate: $1\frac{1}{2}d.$ for the first ounce.

1920*   June 1—Inland rate: 2*d.* for 3 ounces.

1922*   May 29—Inland rate: $1\frac{1}{2}d.$ for the first ounce.

1923*   May 14—Inland rate: $1\frac{1}{2}d.$ for 2 ounces.

1931   September 1—United States breaks away from the Anglo-American postal agreement of 1908 by increasing the postage rate to the United Kingdom.

1940*   May 1—Inland rate: $2\frac{1}{2}d.$ for 2 ounces.

1951   June 1—Penny Postage for printed matter ends.
1957   October 1—Great Britain ends the Anglo-American agree-
        ment of 1908, by rating letters to the United States the
        same as for foreign countries.
   * Inland rate: increased to 3*d.* for 1 ounce.
   * indicates changes in Inland postal rates in Great Britain.

Bibliography

THE PENNY POST 1680–1918

The History of the King's Messengers, V. WHEELER-HOLOHAN (Grayson)

The King's Messengers, 1199–1377, MARY C. HILL (Edward Arnold)

The Pastons and their England, H. S. BENNETT (Cambridge)

William Dockwra and the Rest of the Undertakers, T. TODD (Cousland)

Origins of the Penny Post, FRED J. MELVILLE

John Wildman, Plotter and Postmaster, MAURICE ASHLEY (Jonathan Cape)

History of the Post Office, HERBERT JOYCE (Bentley)

The History of the British Post Office, HEMMEON (Harvard)

Britain's Post Office, HOWARD ROBINSON (Oxford)

Royal Mail, F. GEORGE KAY (Rockliff)

The Jubilee of Penny Postage, 1890 (G.P.O.)

The Endless Webb (John Dickinson & Co.), JOAN EVANS (Jonathan Cape)

Fifty Years of Public Life, SIR HENRY COLE

The Life and Letters of Sir John Henniker Heaton, Bart., MRS. ADRIAN (PORTER Bodley Head)

Life of Sir Rowland Hill, JOHN BIRKBECK HILL (De la Rue & Co.)

Elihu Burritt, His Life and Labours, C. NORTHEND (Sampson Low)

The Learned Blacksmith, MERLE CURTIS (Wilson-Erikson Inc.)

The Centenary of Penny Postage (The Postal History Society)

The Postmarks of Gt. Britain and Ireland, ALCOCK & HOLLAND (Alcock)

Early Days of the Sun Fire Office, EDWARD BAUMER (Sir Joseph Causton & Sons)

History of the Christmas Card, GEORGE BUDAY (Rockliff)

Histoire de la Poste aux Lettres et du Timbre Postes, A. ROTHSCHILD (1879)

Etude sur les Messageries et les Postes, FLORANGE (1925)

Scott's Specialized United States Stamp Catalogue

The Development of Rates of Postage, A. D. SMITH (Allen & Unwin)

The Ninth Report of the Commissioners on the Post Office, 1837 (H.M. Stationery Office)

PAMPHLETS AND ARTICLES

Post Office Reform (1837), ROWLAND HILL
Ashurst's Facts (1838), W. H. ASHURST
Hunt's Merchant's Magazine (New York, 1840)
Uniform Imperial Postage, R. J. BEADEN, M.A. (Cassell, 1891)
St. Martin's-le-Grand (The Post Office Magazine), Vols. 1 to 21
The Philatelist, Vol. 17, Nos. 4 to 9 (Pub. Robson Lowe Ltd.)
The Local Posts of London, GEORGE BRUMELL
The Bulletin, No. 49, "Peter Williamson's Post", SIR WALTER MERCER (The Postal History Society)

Index